the social entrepreneur

Andrew Mawson's career in the social sector has
spanned over 20 years. He developed the renowned
Bromley-by-Bow Centre in East London and co-
founded the Community Action Network in 1998. He
is currently involved in developing London's Water
City. He was awarded a Life Peerage in 2007 and in
the same year was named in the *Evening Standard*
as one of London's most influential people.

THE
# socialentrepreneur

## MAKING COMMUNITIES WORK

# ANDREW MAWSON

Atlantic Books
LONDON

First published in trade paperback in Great Britain in 2008 by
Atlantic Books, an imprint of Grove/Atlantic Ltd.

3 5 7 9 8 7 5

A CIP catalogue record for this book is available from
the British Library.

978 1 84354 661 0

Printed in Great Britain by MPG Books Ltd, Bodmin, Cornwall

Atlantic Books
An imprint of Grove Atlantic Ltd
Ormond House
26–27 Boswell Street
London
WC1N 3JZ

*For Susan*

*Our children, Liam, Fern and Angel*

*And our staff and friends at the Bromley-by-Bow Centre
who have shared this journey with us*

# Contents

List of illustrations  xi

Foreword  xv

Introduction  1

Bromley-by-Bow  15

Accepting the challenge  129

Twelve steps towards an entrepreneurial future  161

What next for East London?  171

Further reading and resources  179

Acknowledgements  187

The Road goes ever on and on
Down from the door where it began.
Now far ahead the Road has gone,
And I must follow, if I can,
Pursuing it with eager feet,
Until it joins some larger way,
When many paths and errands meet.
And whither then? I cannot say.

J.R.R. Tolkien
*The Lord of the Rings*

# list of illustrations

Andrew Mawson and family in 1984 (Bromley-by-Bow Centre archive)

The archway before restoration (Bromley-by-Bow Centre archive)

Ethel with donated bus (Bromley-by-Bow Centre archive)

The church hall after conversion to nursery (Ros Smith, Wyatt MacLaren Architects)

Santiago Bell in his workshop with one of his sculptures (Barclays PLC)

The church hall set up for worship (Gordon MacLaren, Wyatt MacLaren LLP)

The other side of Bromley-by-Bow (Bromley-by-Bow Centre archive)

The derelict park before redesign and landscaping (Bromley-by-Bow Centre archive)

Tessa Jowell with Andrew Mawson and the Bromley-by-Bow team at the opening of the medical centre in 1998 (Lorenzo Lees)

View of the park as it is today (Gordon MacLaren, Wyatt MacLaren LLP)

Andrew Mawson with the Prince of Wales in 1995 (Lorenzo Lees)

The architect's plans for the centre (Gordon MacLaren, Wyatt MacLaren LLP)

A note from Tony Blair to Andrew Mawson (Author archive)

Andrew Mawson meets Tony Blair in 1995 (Lorenzo Lees)

A mosaic by Sheenagh McKinlay (Gordon MacLaren, Wyatt MacLaren LLP)

The front courtyard as it is today (Gordon MacLaren, Wyatt MacLaren LLP)

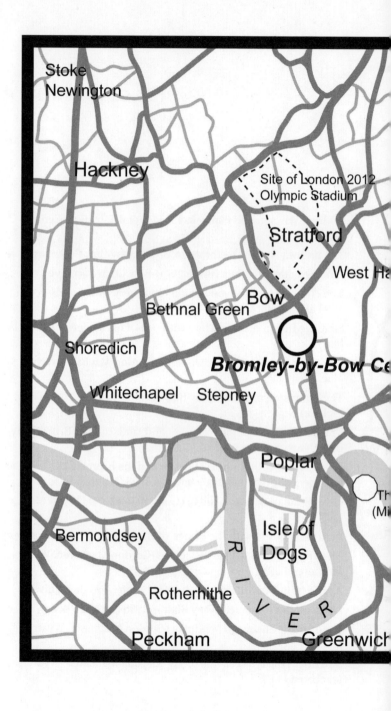

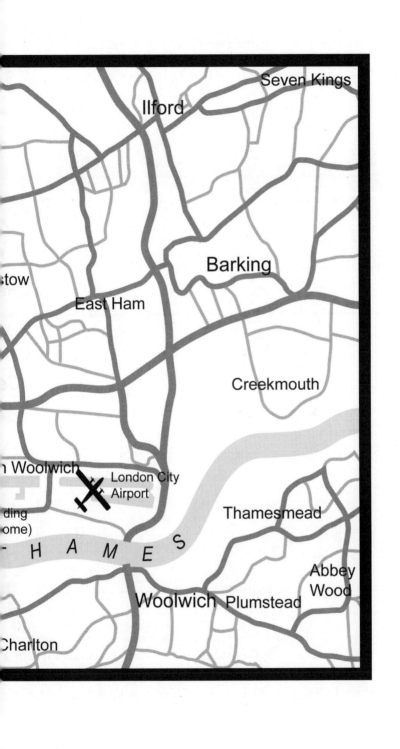

# foreword

I write this book, deliberately, as a polemic. I argue passionately for a particular entrepreneurial approach to achieving social goals which questions the liberal consensus, and I do so based on my experience of over twenty years working in one of the most historically socially 'failing' parts of the country, Bromley-by-Bow in London's East End. I pose a direct challenge to the prevailing approaches and attitudes of policy makers, politicians, social commentators, journalists, the civil service and the charitable (or 'third') sector in order to encourage and open up a debate about how we might finally get to grips with this country's most deeply entrenched social problems and make real, lasting change for generations to come.

Please note that some names have been changed to protect the identity of certain members of the community in Bromley-by-Bow.

# introduction

As a young man I was bought up on a diet of liberal theological education, the virtues of philanthropy and a healthy suspicion of business. Twenty-four years later the realities of working at the heart of some of Britain's poorest estates had turned me into a social entrepreneur, committed to applying business principles to social issues.

The term 'social entrepreneur' first appeared in the UK in an article in the *Independent* in June 1995 referring to me and my colleague Adele Blakebrough. We were part of the small group of individuals who founded the social entrepreneur movement in the United Kingdom, before we even had a term to describe who we were and what we did. Nowadays, the term 'social entrepreneur' is frequently bandied about and I fear it is in danger of coming to mean different things to different people. I want to shed light on what social entrepreneurship is all about and who social entrepreneurs are – to lay out what sets apart this entrepreneurial way of working from what has gone before and show how it challenges many of our current assumptions about the provision of public services within Western democracies. I do not want to develop such a tight definition that all creativity is precluded – indeed, creativity lies at the very heart of any definition of the term – but I do want to make a clear distinction between the traditional approach of the state and charitable sectors on the one hand and the approach of people with a more entrepreneurial mindset on the other.

I want to show how we might all embrace this new way of working. Because this is a genuine attempt to get to the heart of a serious problem I will have to tell some uncomfortable truths along the way. If human creativity and a commitment to changing the world remains at the core of social entrepreneurship, people's aspirations for social change can be turned into realistic, practical action on the ground in their neighbourhoods, on their streets. It truly does make a difference.

Social entrepreneurs worth their salt do not follow conventional ways of working. Their view of the world begins with people, passion, experience and story – not policy, statistics and theory. One of the methods they use to animate a given environment is to challenge people to metaphorically 'rearrange the furniture' in ways that unsettle, challenge and confront them. I hope that this book will have a similar effect.

In my own work, I have quite consciously gone into failing situations to shake things up. This immediately stands me apart from the crowd and draws attention to my message. In this way I have found that I can quickly draw kindred spirits to my campaign. This approach is far more effective when building a team than placing a *Guardian* advert. Playing the *enfant terrible* is in fact very purposeful. It can really bring a situation to life and remind people that nothing is actually fixed in their world, that change really is possible.

In my own tradition of the Christian church, this methodology of dissent and challenge is well known, but often overlooked. The prophet Ezekiel, for example, alone dared to suggest that all was not well within his society. Social entrepreneurs belong to this 'left field' tradition, representatives of which can be found in ancient and modern cultures throughout history and across the world. Time and again they are the *real* agents of change. The nonconformist churches in Britain, which were built in the main by dissenters, have now to a large degree been taken over by conformists who talk endlessly about 'making poverty history' but are not prepared to do the hard work or embrace the business logic necessary to do anything really practical and to scale about it. This is with some notable exceptions, of course, and where they exist they are often impressive. Eric Blakebrough, for example, my early mentor and a Baptist minister at that time, founded the Kaleidoscope Project in Kingston-upon-Thames to challenge the prevailing views in the sixties and seventies about drug abuse and has given a lifetime of service to this often neglected community.

Social entrepreneurs know from hard-won experience that the trick is first to demonstrate what you are proposing to do for people in a small and tangible way and then to expand the sense of possibility. What you say and do really matters to people: seeing is believing. Integrity is the name of the game. Social entrepreneurs are not being difficult for its – or their – own sake. They seek to change the ethos within which people live and work and create paradigm shifts. They seek to initiate change at a number of different levels at the same time, thus creating momentum. Jamie Oliver offered us a great example of this in his 2005 *School Dinners* television series. Not only did he run a very successful campaign, he also demonstrated a way of working which bought profound change to one of London's poorest communities.

Jamie did not begin with the think tanks, committees and research documents so often favoured by civil servants and politicians. He began with the inner dynamics of a very human situation, with the head dinner lady, Nora, and her school kitchen at Kidbrooke Comprehensive in south-east London. Innovation in public service did not come via the usual processes of government: it came through building strong relationships with Nora and her team of dinner ladies, and by observing and coming to really understand the daily inner dynamics of a school kitchen. This was the 'theatre': together they had to write the play.

Jamie is an animator. We watched as he inspired the dinner ladies to get back in touch with the passion for food and cookery that had brought them to the school meal business in the first place. He then went further, engaging with the children and their parents, the head teacher, the local education authority, and eventually central government and the Prime Minister. Jamie Oliver almost unwittingly developed an approach to working with people which conferred on him real legitimacy. Millions of people across Britain supported him. Many of our politicians would give their right arms to have such popular backing. He became credible, of course, not because of what committees he chaired or sat on, not by whom he claimed to represent, but by what he actually did. This is the classic 'inside-out' approach of the social entrepreneur, which begins with people and the building blocks of human relationships.

Jamie demonstrated a way of tackling a social problem

that fundamentally challenged the prevailing orthodoxy. I would wager that, had it been allowed to mature over a period of some years, it might have brought directly quantifiable change to Kidbrooke; it might have changed the social and political landscape and achieved in practice, in a poor inner-city area apparently firmly resistant to 'change', what New Labour and David Cameron's Conservatives have so often talked about rhetorically but have so rarely achieved. But this was a television series, a piece of entertainment. This early innovation in school meals has now been handed back to government, to the very same structures and methodology that contributed to the problem of poor-quality food in the first place.

Government created a representative committee, the School Meals Review Panel, to take the project forward. They made recommendations. They were followed by the Schools Food Trust. They have been concerned to make this a national project but in my view this very focus on the national aims, rather than the local ones, have stopped any real innovation dead in its tracks. Yes, the food may improve in schools across the country; millions of pounds of public money will be spent to ensure it does. The chips might be replaced by sautéed potatoes, but the real possibility for innovation which Jamie Oliver's series demonstrated – the opportunity for long-term change in a difficult inner-city area – has been lost. It was lost when government failed to grasp the implications of a more entrepreneurial, organic way of working, which enabled one person to be a change maker and did not compartmentalize human creativity. Once again, government puts its trust in and gives its backing to structures, rather than individuals.

Social entrepreneurs often defy easy definition. When you think you have them neatly placed in a box, like Houdini they find a way out – for we are, by nature, creative spirits. However, I think it is possible to identify some commonly shared principles – in particular our concern to apply business experience and business logic to social questions.

'Learning by doing' – this is a phrase we associate with children and childhood. I recently watched my young son struggling to put together the four pieces of a Noddy jigsaw. His first two attempts were very frustrating. There were tears and a bid to leave the room. But we persevered and on attempt number three, as if by magic, the pieces all fitted into place. Success! I came home a month later to find that he'd put together a hundred-piece jigsaw puzzle on his own. I recount the story because I think it illustrates very well a 'can-do' approach to tackling what seemed, to my son, to be an insurmountable problem. Had government been enlisted to help my son out with his problem, here's what my experience tells me they'd have done: they'd have set up a committee to assess the situation, full of highly educated people who had probably never put a jigsaw together, but who knew all the theory behind it. They would spend a long time examining the pieces before writing an extensive and expensive report on their findings. They would present this to my son. They would tell him, also, that a policy paper would be forthcoming, which would explore what could be learned from his struggle to put the pieces together and what measures could be taken to 'move forward together'. At no point would they think to simply join him, take hold of the physical pieces of the jigsaw and get stuck in and help him figure things out. Their approach would seem to value the 'bigger picture' more than it would value finding practical, detailed solutions to an urgent problem. The result, for my son at any rate, would be: nothing. He would be left exactly where he had been in the first place, with a lot of pieces and no idea of how to do the puzzle. He'd feel frustrated and he'd feel paralysed. Paralysis by analysis.

The 'learning by doing' approach is the tried and tested approach of the social entrepreneur. We call into question the systems and processes of government, which are still run by well-qualified civil servants who rarely get hold of the pieces themselves and whose approach has so failed many of our poorest communities.

What marks out social entrepreneurs from business entrepreneurs and other kinds of charitable and public-sector workers is that they are not driven solely by financial profit or ideology, or by a career or a pension scheme. Instead they are often driven by a desire to make their mark on the world. They feel they have something important to share that must be demonstrated both emotionally and practically. In my experience they care a lot about people and are talented at forming relationships and creating committed teams and communities around them. They are very serious about learning from, and applying business experience and ideas to, social questions. They are fundamentally interested in what works in practice and how you scale up ideas to achieve effective growth. They are often not easy people to be around, particularly if you are not interested in what they are doing. They are very focused.

The Artic explorer Robert Swan, the first man to walk to both Poles, once told me that the people he chose to join him on his journey were not the suave, mild-mannered people so often favoured to run public-sector bodies: they were rough diamonds who had a real passion for their field and who, when you joined them together with the right team, were capable of getting you there and back alive, with enough to eat and still some to spare. Those are the kinds of people who make good social entrepreneurs. They are like nails: the harder you hit them, the further they go in.

Social entrepreneurs have discovered that business has a considerable amount to teach them. They like business because businesses operate in the real world: if you don't sell your products, you go bust very quickly. The public and charitable sectors often don't have to operate in this 'real' environment – they often stay safely removed, preferring to engage more with theory than practical reality, locked into a grant-dependent culture. Like social entrepreneurs, many business people are passionate, driven people who care deeply about their companies. For many, this is not simply a nine-to-five job: it can be their life's work. Social entrepreneurs are often very serious about social innovation and leaders in the field often have sky-high aspirations; they are literally committed to changing the world.

There have clearly been other periods of social innovation in British history and some of the ideas and approaches of the social entrepreneur are not 'new' ones. The Victorian age famously spawned great philanthropists like William Booth, William Wilberforce, Lord Shaftesbury and countless others who challenged the status quo in their own lifetimes and sought to draw attention to poverty in their society and its destructive effects on human lives. In *Great Expectations* and his other great social novels, Charles Dickens used his remarkable talents as a writer to challenge and transform people's views and inspire compassion and action by communicating a story about the poverty and social inequality he saw around him every single day. Many of the great Victorians knew a thing or two about the more practical approaches I've been talking about. Great engineers like Stevenson and Brunel changed the face of Britain not through policy papers but through engaging with very practical problems over a long period of time. Samuel Lister surely changed the face of the woollen industry from his mill in my home town of Bradford, with his many ingenious patents, but he also changed the prospects, infrastructure and identity of a particular region. One member of his family business told me that officials who visited the mill when Lister was alive often complained that they could never find him in his office – he was invariably under the machinery on the shop floor, mending it or inventing a simple adjustment to make it run more efficiently. These great entrepreneurs stayed loyal to their passions and worried endlessly about the details of their projects in a never-ending drive to make things work better.

They also knew about the value of the long view. John Harrison, for example, devoted a costly lifetime's work to his quest to calculate exact longitude. He knew this level of commitment was necessary if he wanted to understand enough of the practical detail of his art to achieve success. And, of course, the lasting impact of his clock, which saved sailors from the perils of the high seas and changed the world for ever, is beyond measure. I believe that when it comes to some of our most intractable social problems, it is time once again to identify, understand, support and reward people who take a long view and who focus on the practical details of a particular situation and place. We need to back those individuals who commit their lives to these challenging issues rather than being dazzled by fly-by-nights (be they politicians, or journalists, or charity workers) who produce many fine words but few practical solutions. It is time to embrace the world of the social entrepreneur.

What marks out the present phase of social innovation as being significantly different is the developing relationship between social entrepreneurs and business. The terms 'social' and 'entrepreneur' seem to be contradictory. Traditionally they have defined very different worlds: the worlds of community and social life, and the demanding, cut-throat world of business. Social entrepreneurs have recognized, however, that new ideas generally emerge from the creative process that occurs when people from different backgrounds with different approaches engage effectively with each other. Difference and diversity, not conformity and equality, are the fertile soil of social change, the seedbed of new ways of working. Traditional political and governmental processes have failed to understand and embrace this creative new world. The modern worlds of business entrepreneurship and social entrepreneurship are coming to understand this, while the public sector is struggling to catch up and, in the process, often stalling this logic of change.

All of this moves many of us beyond traditional philanthropy into more sustainable models of public service, which have innovation and consumer focus at their core. Those social entrepreneurs who are serious players have seen through the weaknesses of philanthropy and the dangers of its grant-dependent culture in poor communities.

They have experienced the over-dependence on government funding and are attempting to cut themselves free from a world in which everyone is responsible for everything yet, in practice, often no one is responsible for anything or accountable to anyone.

The real clues to how we can refresh our democracy and our participation within it, which so many of our politicians yearn for but never achieve, may not be found in the corridors of Westminster, in debates about the constitution, or through the latest IT gizmo or technology, but by looking more carefully at some of this practical work. I have learned this in my own experience, from people who have stayed the course and created real participation and change in communities – not through a three-year government programme but over perhaps a quarter of a century of emotional and actual investment in a place and the people there. Many answers to macro-political questions must be sought in the micro-experience of local activity, as any business person will tell you. You have to start with one high-street shop and understand its inner workings before you build a thousand. Governments seem to believe that you can build a thousand schools if you have the correct policy framework before they properly understand the practical inner workings of just one.

A few years ago I was invited to speak at a conference in Melbourne, Australia organized by the World Health Organization (WHO). I expected there to be three hundred people there; I was greeted by nearly three thousand, all of whom were working in some of the poorest areas of the world. I listened to four days of speeches by politicians, policy makers and aspiring academics talking about poverty, health and the demands of a planet with ever-diminishing resources and an apparent environmental nightmare about to unravel.

I was asked to give the final keynote address. I went up to the lectern and began by telling the assembled audience that I thought this had been a very well-organized conference. Yet I had spent four days looking at large graphs and hearing about policies for change and endless statistics from around the world. No one had actually mentioned anyone with a name and address. The messy details of people's real lives and experiences were startlingly absent from the platform. I then told our Bromley-by-Bow story, which I will share in this book, and unexpectedly received a standing ovation. I don't think this had anything to do with my abilities as a public speaker. I think it had everything to do with touching a raw nerve and daring to suggest that the way we think about government and its relationship to people, both in Britain and across the world, is profoundly out of kilter with the realities of life experienced by millions of people.

Listening to tales from Bangladesh, India, China and from within the Aboriginal community in Australia, one of the wealthiest countries on earth, alerted me to the massive scale of the problems we are facing. In an increasingly global environment we have to find new ways of learning to live together which are both practical and creative. The way to address issues of race might not be through Downing Street seminars attended by predominantly male religious leaders; it might, though, be about encouraging cross-cultural relationships built around people 'doing' things together. Rewarding those who bother to get off their backsides to work together on practical projects and discouraging those who want to take the lazy, pontificating, seminar-attending approach. My experience has been that when you do this, a wide circle of friends emerge who span the globe and whose common ground is not race but action.

If the new global environment is to work, governments themselves have to become more 'people friendly', more responsive to their electorates, turning their passions and responsibilities into effective and constructive action at a local level. The British government has to actually unpack the contradictions that exist at present in its endless rhetoric about democracy and delivery. It has to drill into the detail, understand the practical contradictions and become far more willing to embrace people and skills as part of the solution. Old ideologies that talk too easily about fairness, social justice and equality need to be challenged and the detailed consequences of these words need to be viewed in practice on the ground. We need to look into the inner workings of the health service, for example, and into the massive wastage of lottery funds, and try to better understand them from a practitioner's point of view. We have to find new ways of using scarce resources, and populations have to be persuaded that they can make a real difference and create for themselves this necessary change, without waiting on the dead hand of government.

The present times present huge challenges for citizens and governments across the world. Governments are profoundly failing both local communities and the planet, and people know it but are at a loss to know what to do about it. They sense that the inner logic of these systems needs to be taken apart and put back together – but how? How do you make the relationship between government and the individual more real and meaningful? Social entrepreneurs are fundamentally optimistic about the world. Where many people see only problems, they see opportunities for change, even in the most challenging and apparently imposing of situations. They demand we see problems afresh, live with apparently impenetrable details and gradually discern the raw materials with which to create practical and sustainable solutions. The challenge they pose to us all is that we commit the time and energy, and sometimes pay the personal price, that social change demands. I hope that this book may suggest some fresh and challenging ways into the puzzles we all face today.

BROMLEY-BY-BOW

# uncertain beginnings

first arrived in Bromley-by-Bow one cold November evening in 1984, to be greeted by twelve people, all over seventy years of age, sitting before me in a two-hundred-seat United Reformed church. I had recently agreed to minister to this congregation after a pastor who was taking the service on one Sunday had suddenly dropped dead in the middle of a liturgy. I felt strongly that all of my theological training to date had been equipping me for this work in the inner cities. But as I stood at the pulpit in the freezing church hall that evening, and after the service as I stood in the derelict gents' loo (which boasted the only cold running water tap in the building), the reality of the situation began to bite and I couldn't help but wonder what on earth I'd got myself into.

I soon realized that I had three clear choices. Stay in bed every morning and become very depressed; hide away in my room and write a doctorate on inner city poverty; or wander the streets, observe the local community and try to understand what on earth was going on outside the solid oak doors that, until now, had protected me from the world.

The first option was a very real one: I had been told about a number of fellow clergy who had 'come off their trolleys', sometimes in spectacular ways. As for option number two, I had watched too many clergy returning from Latin America to write lengthy theses on liberation theology and Third World poverty, all of which would have little or no real effect. So my course was clear – nosey Yorkshireman that I am, I would get to know the people, walk the streets, visit the markets and schools and businesses, become familiar with the area and try to get a handle on what was happening in this community to keep it from fulfilling its potential.

This community in Bromley was built around a group of rundown housing estates, dissected by motorways, which most people chose to forget or simply drove straight past. I soon realized that fifty languages and dialects were spoken within ten minutes' walk of the church building. I also quickly discovered that anyone who could get away had apparently done just that. I was living in a community that showed some of the highest indices of poverty in the UK, and in which one third of the local population seemed trapped in a cycle which had them moving in and out of the estates every three years. Countless government schemes had been tried out in the area over the decades but these had made little apparent difference.

I recently found a map drawn up by William Booth, the founder of the Salvation Army. He had walked these same streets just over a hundred years earlier in 1898, colouring in on a carefully drawn-up plan of the area the shades and gradients of poverty he witnessed street by street. Coventry Cross estate, just up the road, was coloured in dark grey. It was clearly then, as it was back in 1984, one of the bleakest parts of London. Little had changed, despite the countless social programmes to solve the problem, and I was worried that the area seemed destined to be forever regarded as a 'social problem' – a 'thing' to waste words on but have few real hopes for. The scale of the task I faced was dizzying.

To ease my anxiety I began searching for clues about what I could do to help. I began with the Anglican 'Faith in the City' report, which had just been published, and which outlined the Church's 'Urban Priority Areas' and looked at what might be done to alleviate problems faced by those inner-city parishes. At the time, Mrs Thatcher presented it as further evidence of the church's decline into socialism (which she, of course, found most unhelpful). My own concerns about it were more practical. To me, it seemed to be a document full of pious academic theory about the poor, thrashed out in the senior common rooms of theological colleges and British universities by people who had never built or actually changed anything in their lives. There were only three pages at the back of the book that gave me anything resembling a practical suggestion as to what I could do. I threw it in the bin. The only route that made any sense to me was to hang around, meet some local people and try and get my head around what was actually going on here, on the ground.

One of the first people I got to know was Lillian, the church caretaker who lived conveniently just across the road with her husband Ted. Ted was a former docker who carried a large chip on his shoulder against the clergy and anything religious. He had lived through the decline of the docks and the rise of the trade unions and had become understandably cynical towards anyone who offered to do anything for him and his community. He had seen it all come and go, and nothing had changed yet.

I walked into the empty church buildings on my second day, and had been there for less than five minutes when I noticed Lillian appear and begin to quietly sweep the church hall floor. It occurred to me that the floor, though old, was actually perfectly clean: after all, I was the only person who had been there for weeks – besides the church hall, the buildings were only used once a month, for Labour Party meetings. Perhaps she was keeping an eye on me? I began to feel that I was an intruder, that maybe I was invading her space, her sanctuary. I approached her and we began a conversation. She offered to take me on a tour around the rundown buildings, show me the place. I agreed.

The first room we visited she described as the 'Boys' Brigade rifle room'. The windows had been bricked up many years earlier, and the room was pitch black; but I sensed a long oblong space before me, and I could most certainly feel the seepage of water underfoot and smell the damp papers and furniture that lay somewhere out there, as I stood straining to see into the dark. As I groped for a light switch, an excited little voice behind me shouted, 'Don't switch on the lights, you'll get electrocuted!'

I paddled my way across the long, narrow room, avoiding obstacles by following the wall. Eventually I reached the back of the room and, to my surprise, felt the familiar shape of a piano. The timid voice behind me chirped up again, 'I polish it every Thursday.' I lifted the lid and tried to press the keys: they were stiff solid.

It struck me then that Lillian, unrecognized by anyone, was working out her life on the building. Lillian exemplified a number of people who I would come to meet over the years in the area who lived on the edges of mental ill health.

These people were often desperately isolated and worked out their loneliness or frustrations through deep attachments to someone, or something else – in Lillian's case, her routine of cleaning the church buildings. These people are too frequently hidden from the view of state-funded professional caring agencies. What Lillian needed – relied on – was a community within which she could have a role and be valued. Written reports and expensive medication, certainly in isolation, were of little or no help to her sense of worth as an individual, a human being. As I stood with Lillian in that dark, damp room, looking down at the woefully neglected piano, I realized just how deeply we all depend for our sanity on relationships with other people. They give us our sense of reality and equilibrium. Without them we all stumble.

During the coming months I came to know a few more local people. By chance I came across Su who lived in a rundown short-life property four doors away from the church ('short life' is a term common in east London – it means 'short let'). She shared the house with another tenant, Ebon, a passionate gardener who had converted their back garden into a fantastic tropical greenhouse, full of exotic and fragrant plants growing under a makeshift plastic bubble, in which visitors to their home luxuriated. I was reminded of this dome when I recently visited the Eden Project in Cornwall, but back then it struck me as a wholly unexpected and remarkable breath of life and colour in the middle of such a grey and impoverished borough. Here, I began to see, behind closed doors and in people's passions and skills, there was real beauty to be found. Far from being a lost cause, I was beginning to have a sense of real hope and ambition.

Su and Ebon invited me around one day, and we sat for ages sipping tea and ruminating on the ills of the world. The docklands and Canary Wharf had not yet been built at this stage and property in east London was still very cheap. The few remaining terraced houses that the bombs had not destroyed were rich pickings for artistically inclined young people who had decided to drop out of the rat race. The new young clergyman who had appeared on the corner was an intriguing prospect, and Su and Ebon wanted to know more about me – did I have anything to offer, or was I a bit of a joke? Would I simply confirm all their worst fears about the Church and religion in general?

There was one thing that I could, potentially, offer. Su, it seemed, was into boat-building in a big way and was keen to use my empty hall to build a small sailing dinghy. A great idea I thought – no one else was using it. I explained that I would have to discuss this matter with the twelve attending parishioners. The United Reformed Church functions as a democracy and they, as Elders, would have to decide whether or not this could be allowed. In my mind's eye I could already see Lillian appearing with her broom one morning, worried silly about all the mess it would create. Su looked quizzical; she clearly thought it was a rather quaint idea.

Two weeks later at the next church meeting, as we gathered around the heater with the pilot light shedding its customary glow (but still no actual warmth), I explained Su's proposition. There followed a discussion about 'those strange young people' who were currently living in the houses next door to where dear Alice Wood had lived with her family all her life. Could Su be trusted with a key to the building? Ethel, who was wearing the usual warm grey woolly hat, was intrigued. This cheerful East End grandmother was seventy-three years old in body and seventeen years old in spirit. I was already beginning to love her sense of fun, her openness and her clarity of thought. We would one day name a block of flats after her but at this point I was only just getting to know her. She came to my rescue with an inspiring and persuasive argument. 'Noah built a boat and so why shouldn't Su?' Exactly! The decision was made and it was unanimous.

# building a boat

**W**ithin days Su began to move her timber into the empty hall and as the materials began to stack up at the far end of the room I began to see a rather obvious problem arising. Once Su had built the boat in the hall, how on earth was she going to get it out again through that small door? To my relief, Su had actually thought about this, and had designed the vessel so that it could be taken apart and removed piece by piece when it was eventually finished. I began to discover that this young and creative woman was as sharp as a tack and far more mature than her tender years suggested.

Two completely different generations now inhabited the same space – my church hall – even though to date they had never actually met or spoken to each other. Together, we had all unwittingly made a small step forward.

As Su began carefully to build the boat, I decided I needed to establish a rhythm to my own working day as a means of remaining sane so that my time had some purpose and structure besides 'getting to know' people and places. In the mornings, then, I would go around and meet people, intro-duce myself to the head teacher, the local doctor, members of the voluntary sector and so forth. In the afternoons I would go back to the church and try for an hour each day to teach myself the piano. My target was Grade One in six months' time (which was made much more difficult on an instrument whose middle 'C' did not actually work). It was certainly no easy task, but I persevered and eventually passed Grade 1 with distinction.

This detour each afternoon meant that I would meet Su most days. I was getting to know her a lot better, and I was also becoming more conscious of who came in and out of the buildings each day. Occasionally Ethel would come round for a cup of tea to make preparations for her old ladies' group, which now met once a week. She would say hello to Su and watch with interest as the 'ark' began to take shape.

About six weeks into the project Ethel came up to me one day and declared, 'I saw Su down the Roman Road market yesterday, she's a really nice girl you know.' I agreed. Within a matter of days Su also stopped me. 'I really like Ethel,' she said, as though she'd made a big discovery, 'she has a great sense of humour. And I love the woolly hat!' A connection had been made between the generations, a bridge had been crossed, and I felt that I was no longer alone.

Two weeks later I arrived in the hall early one morning to find the boat all but finished and a small Maxwell House coffee jar full of wild flowers by the far wall. A note had been carefully placed alongside the flowers: 'Wild flowers of Bow, with many thanks, Su.'

# building relationships

The first person who came to the church, wanting to become a member of my small and largely elderly congregation, was Linda, a supremely gentle middle-class lady. At the end of her first service with us she had been accosted by Jenny, the self-taught church organist, with the words, 'You're not going to try and get off with my husband John, are you?' John, by the way, was well into his fifties, totally loyal and by every count the last person you would ever imagine having a fling. Equally, Linda's first marriage had failed and she had had enough of men to last her a lifetime. I rather felt we existed in a time warp – or some parallel dimension – behind the large oak doors, and I must admit that I secretly feared for any new people wanting to assimilate into our world.

But the second person who turned up at the church and wanting to join was Doreen. Doreen was a very traditional East End mother with a huge smile, and she was well rounded in every sense. She had been drawn to the church because she wanted to introduce her first child, Christopher, to the traditions of Christianity. She wanted the best for her kids and I suspect she thought that I was one route in to what she saw as a better life. Doreen was a tough cookie and she dealt with Jenny's challenging accusations on a friendly yet firm basis.

'Jenny's a bit unusual,' she said to me with a wink, after the second service she attended.

'I know,' I said, trying not to smile.

A few weeks later, as I sat in Doreen's tenement flat, sharing coffee and swapping jokes, I told her about the ecumenical service I had recently organized at the large Catholic Church further down the borough in Poplar. I described how I had used this occasion to introduce Jenny and my elderly Protestant members to the sign of the Peace, a long-held Catholic tradition. I wanted to bring this small piece of liturgical innovation into our Sunday service and I thought that this would be a good opportunity for them to experience it at first hand. After the apparently successful service, Jenny had come up to me and said, "Ere, during that Peace thing a woman came up to me and shook my hand and said, "May the sun shine up your garden path". Well, what else could I say,' said Jenny, 'but "And up yours!"' Doreen split her sides and we both realized we had an entertainer in our midst.

As more people appeared in the buildings the cleaning duties became too much for Lillian, so Doreen agreed to take them on. Running around the church hall with a broom and an oversized floor polisher was no easy task for a very large lady, but she persevered. One Sunday I arrived at the hall to find Doreen looking acutely embarrassed and upset. I enquired what the matter was. Apparently her husband, Ken, had taken her keys for the church without her knowing and was coming to the buildings late at night. He had been using the telephone in my office without permission, apparently to make dodgy telephone calls. His method was to dial any series of numbers that came into his head. He could not read or write, so was unable to use the phone book, but if a woman answered his call he would promise her the world and offer to meet. Unfortunately, the previous week he had by chance dialled the reception at Bow Road police station. Not the brightest tool in the box, when the pleasant young woman who had answered his call had willingly agreed to take him up on his offer, Ken had eagerly arranged to meet her outside the station. He had been duly arrested and charged, leaving poor Doreen in a real state.

These encounters – with Lillian, Ted, Ethel, Su, Doreen and others – all gave me clues and pointers that would eventually allow me to piece together a very intimate picture of what was going on in the lives of the people who lived on these estates. More than that, though, they also told me a great deal about the human potential that lay untapped behind the endless barred-up windows and doors. For me, the way forward was to work with and through the lives of these people I was coming to know and like. This was not 'unpromising material', as some fellow clergy and local liberal commentators had said. These lives were alive with possibility, even to my untrained eye, and I was determined that, by engaging in practical projects together, our little band could grow stronger and make some very important changes.

# investing in dreams

**W**hen Su eventually carefully removed her boat from the hall I was left once again with an empty space. One day, I took a telephone call from a woman named Janet who was looking for somewhere to establish a dance school and was enquiring around local churches to see whether they had any rooms free. I agreed to meet her in the rundown hall the following Saturday morning.

Janet began by telling me that she had been a professional dancer and that she now wanted to build her own studio. She had real drive and a tangible passion for dance, and I knew that simply hiring the space to her, as most churches and voluntary sector organizations do, was not the way forward. To do that would give her the impression that her work was entirely separate from, and nothing to do with, the life of the community, and that was not how I saw things at all. I suggested the following deal: if she agreed to work in partnership with me, I would form a business-like relationship with her. We would work together to try and make the school a success and through it offer local children creative opportunities that they would not otherwise have access to. She would get the school, and I would get a reliable rent cheque and a whole set of new relationships on which I could build. We would learn by doing, together. This was my first attempt to establish a practical response to the needs of local residents.

Janet began to build and develop the school. East End mums are not stupid – they want the best for their children and they instinctively knew that Janet was no fraud. They knew within an instant that Janet was a professional dancer, that she had actually performed, on stage and television, even on cruise ships, and that she knew and could teach the disciplines necessary to get into the dance and media industry. They were happy to pay for her classes.

To my surprise I began to receive complaints from members of the local charitable sector. In their eyes, it seemed, it was unacceptable that these 'poor' parents should have to pay for their children to benefit from the service that Janet was providing. They thought it was capitalism let loose on an unsuspecting East End estate. I argued that I couldn't find any grants, there was no other way for Janet to offer the classes and that, as a matter of fact, it might be a good idea to let these East Enders decide how they wanted to spend their own money. This was a business that had something to offer both parents and children, and I saw it as an encouraging sign that many parents were choosing to invest in opportunities for their children.

Janet continued to build the school, in spite of the opposition, and by year six not only did we have a hundred and fifty children enjoying the classes, we were also running annual shows and events, and one child had even been offered a place at the Royal Ballet School. The gap between those in the voluntary sector who claimed to represent the local community and to know about what local people wanted, and what real people actually chose to do with their own money, seemed to me to be ever widening. How had they become so out of touch with realities on the ground?

# princes into frogs

round this time, in 1986, Mrs Thatcher was encouraging us all to think about the institutions of marriage and the family. I decided that maybe a way to deepen our connections into the estate was to hold a public meeting on precisely this subject and to talk to our neighbours about what marriage meant to them. I dutifully prepared (and had printed at great expense) what I thought was an imaginative A4 leaflet. On the front was a cartoon drawing of a wife with curlers in her hair doing the ironing in front of the television. Her husband was lying back in an armchair with his legs up on a stool, a cigarette in his mouth and a pint of Guinness in his hand. The caption at the top of the leaflet read: 'Marriage is magic; it turns princes into frogs!' On the back was an invitation to join me, not at the church but in a secular community building nearby. I didn't want anyone to see this as yet another religious trick, a means of getting them into the church by the back door.

I spent three days personally hand-delivering all 2000 of the things, running up and down the stairs of countless blocks of flats. I discovered in the process that in the twenty-five-storey blocks the lifts often didn't work and that the elderly residents and the young mums with prams usually lived on the top floors. I became an expert in different-shaped letterboxes and devised many ingenious ways to shove and shuffle leaflets through doors reinforced with complicated prison-like bars. I also got to know which doors had large dogs salivating on the other side, ready to bite my fingers off. I became an expert in deciphering whether the smell on the landings was stale urine, boiled cabbage or (an increasingly popular choice) curry.

I also came to realize that as I delivered my leaflets I was following the paper trail of countless other well-meaning people with something to sell: circulars from the council, the Labour Party, the Liberal Democrats, the evangelical Christians, the Socialist Workers, the Workers Revolutionary Party and countless others. Determined not to be fazed, I dutifully delivered my leaflets fully believing that the 'catchy' design and imaginative strap line would do the trick.

When the evening arrived, only three people turned up – and two of them were church members! Su, true to her spirit, just laughed. It was an important lesson for me in how to waste a lot of time, money and energy. I had walked for miles and not connected with anyone.

# the culture club

The London borough of Tower Hamlets was teeming with small charities. There was a long tradition of charitable work in the East End of London, pioneered by famous names like William Booth, whose social reforms had eventually affected the entire country. Over the years universities had gathered together the writings of these well-known social reformers, and they were used as texts in a number of social, political and theological courses. I myself had learned about social reform from an academic perspective, and believed very much in the liberal values I had gleaned from the pages of books.

My parish, in Bromley-by-Bow, was being overwhelmed by what seemed to be a veritable army of very well-meaning and socially conscious voluntary-sector campaigners, who had all been to university and read the same books as I had, and who had come to the East End to 'do good' to people, believing that they knew what local people wanted, convinced that they could represent the local people's interests.

There was, though, another force to be reckoned with: and in my case it stood, literally facing me, on the other side of the road. Tesco, the supermarket chain, had just built and opened a superstore there. We were being told that predators, like Tesco, were all over the East End, buying up the derelict land on the Isle of Dogs (land which had lain unused for years as the public sector squabbled endlessly about how to use it) and generally strutting their stuff. Tesco represented business, and business, so the formula had it, was here to exploit local people and must be resisted at all costs.

I recognized a religion when I saw it: religion, after all, was my core business and here was a faith fully intact and, unlike me, very active and recruiting members on the streets of east London. Here were two closed circles within which thrived two tribes, and any connection between or any infection from one to the other was fiercely resisted at all costs. The religion was clear, their actions were obvious – campaign and protest.

I was becoming increasingly uneasy with it all, with the distance between the theories I, too, had picked up at university and the impact all this activity would have on the lives of people who lived their lives in the areas that were marked out as the battleground.

The pop group Culture Club were very popular during this period of the 1980s. To me, their name accurately described the army of charity workers I was meeting, who seemed intent on living their lives together in a vacuum, sustained by theory, so confident that they understood the workings of the modern world. I attended endless clergy meetings in which we would discuss the impossibility of changing anything and endlessly 'reflect' on what it all meant. That was until one church retreat in Kent at the old 'Hoppers Hospital', when a Methodist minister and close colleague, John Kennedy, dared to suggest that socialism didn't actually work. That it was actually an engine of poverty. It came like a bolt out of the blue. He then illustrated why he had come to that conclusion, through his experience of working for nearly ten years in Old Ford, the next village down the road from me now. He dared to unpick the comfortable liberal traditions we had all been raised on and, if we were honest, had become complacent about. John had begun to both see and understand the world from Doreen's and Ethel's point of view. It was time to face up to the hypocrisy of my own liberal religion – and dump it. The final trigger came in the form of a building, Kingsley Hall.

# confronting Gandhi

**A**round the corner from my own (now much-improved) church buildings was the newly renovated Kingsley Hall Community Centre. Kingsley Hall is renowned. When Mahatma Gandhi had visited London in 1931 for the Round Table talks on India, he had turned down Churchill's offer of a room at the Savoy and had instead chosen to stay with his Christian Socialist friends Muriel and Doris Lester at Kingsley Hall.

The Lester sisters had moved to the East End some years earlier from Loughton in Essex. They passed through the squalid East End estates every day on their train journeys from Loughton into Central London, and every day they witnessed the hardship faced by pre-Welfare State East Enders. These were people of conscience, and they chose to do something about it, deciding to make it their life's work to improve the lot of the people of the East End. Muriel and Doris Lester moved first into a terrace house at number 60 Bruce Road and one of their first tasks was to build what was one of the first children's nurseries in the country at the end of the street. It was called Children's House.

Their next task was to employ the well-known architect Charles Voysey to design a state-of-the-art community building for local people, which they would name after their recently deceased brother Kingsley. Kingsley Hall would be a high-quality red-brick structure with two flagpoles at its entrance. It would be optimistic in its tone, a statement about a new future which they intended to work with local people to build.

A host of famous names had trodden these streets I was living and working in, and many of them were drawn there by Kingsley Hall nearly half a century earlier. John Galsworthy, author of *The Forsyte Saga*, had planted a tree in the garden there. After his visit, Clement Atlee had invited Muriel to Number 10 Downing Street to discuss her idea of making milk available to young children in every school across the country. And now the formidable Muriel had managed to persuade the great Mahatma to come and stay, having met with him during a trip to India.

Alice Woods, one of my very elderly church members, recounted how she used to get up early to join Gandhi for his early morning walks along the canal with his goat. All the children used to go, she said – she remembered it as though it was yesterday. I heard how the Mahatma lived in a small room at the top of the building which overlooked a small roof garden, and how he would receive visitors from all over the world in this unassuming place. I also heard of the time Charlie Chaplin visited him, and the excitement on the streets when the great entertainer came.

The inside story, however, was told to me by Lylie Valentine, a local woman now well into her eighties who had become a great friend of the Lesters. I first met Lylie through her daughters, Doris and Joy, who still live in the estate. She had been at the Mahatma's side for most of the ten weeks of his visit. When I entered Lylie's small second-floor flat I was immediately drawn to a small hand drawing of Gandhi hanging in her hallway.

Lylie was a bright, straight-talking East Ender who had no time for Mrs Thatcher. She told me about her time with Gandhi. One story that stayed with me was of a local boy who was caned at school for getting back late after lunch; he had been stopped on a street corner by Charlie Chaplin and Mahatma Gandhi, he protested (which insolence probably prolonged the beating). She also described in great detail how Muriel and Doris saw the world and began to express her concerns about what was happening to the hall and how the present incumbents' actions bore very little in common with the Lesters' spirit, though it was being done in their name. I would come to understand exactly what she meant...

After the Lesters died the hall had been handed over to the Philadelphia Society and the psychiatrist R. D. Laing, who used it as a base for his experimental work on the family and schizophrenia. Lylie told me stories of people at this time running naked along the roof; bizarre and wild tales circulated locally describing some of the goings-on. The well-known artist Mary Barnes had lived there at this time and one of her pictures had been found on one of the walls during the hall's renovation many years later.

After Ronnie Laing left, the hall was closed down and gradually fell into a state of dereliction until, some years before I arrived, a group of people had come together to raise the money necessary to reopen the hall as a community centre. Out went the stained glass, the small chapel and the fine finishing that Muriel had been so keen on; in came a management committee with a strong sense that there should be no leaders and that all decisions would now be made democratically, through the committee.

I decided that if I was to be paid to be a local minister I could not justify this stipend if my only task was to serve twelve people, no matter how much I was growing to like them and their ways. I must be a pastor to the neighbourhood as a whole. It was also clear that if good things were going on locally that enriched the community then my task was not to compete with them in the name of the church but to help them grow and develop. Hence my first encounter with Kingsley Hall.

As a way of getting to know people and support Kingsley Hall, I began to help one of the young youth workers, Jean, as she organized a summer events programme. We sat together in a hall with a cross-section of local young people and Jean asked them what they wanted to do. 'Well, Miss', they always called her Miss, 'we want to go to Walton-on-the-Naze, ice skating and horse riding.' Dutifully we all trooped onto the buses supplied by Empress Coaches (an East End institution).

When the summer programmes series was over, we all gathered again at the hall and, once again, Jean asked these young people what they wanted to do. 'Well, Miss, Walton-on-the-Naze, horse riding and ice skating,' came the reply.

'Why are you asking these young people such a ridiculous question?' I asked.

'I'm asking the people what they want,' she said.

'This is ridiculous,' I responded. 'These young people have only ever been to three places, they have only ever tasted three bottles of wine on the shelves at Tesco's. They don't know anything else. You've been lucky enough to be a student; you've travelled to Australia and seen a lot of the world. Why don't you suggest that we take them across the Sinai desert in eight months' time?'

'Don't be ridiculous,' was the reply. 'They have never heard of the Sinai desert.'

'Precisely!'

In later years we would take over two hundred young people across the Sinai desert. When we returned from these trips and asked them, again, what they were interested in doing next time round, they never mentioned Walton-on-the-Naze. One of this original group, Darren, won a Churchill Fellowship and studied youth work in the United States and has now travelled all around Australia under his own steam. Others have gone on to set up their own enterprises: all of them can see and imagine a life far beyond the Lea Valley ice rink.

The lesson was this: if you ask an East Ender who is used to using a mangle what they want, they will say a super-mangle; but the fledgling social entrepreneur in me was desperate to show them the spin dryer! I knew, as did local people when I eventually pointed it out, that to understand what a community like ours needed, we had to look at something more complicated than simply asking people what they wanted. As any business entrepreneur could have told us, people often do not necessarily know what they want. The way in to people's real needs and aspirations would require imagination, daring and a massive creative leap.

Jean, the youth worker, was limiting their horizons by offering them the equivalent of a Tesco's choice of three bottles of cheap wine. It was becoming clear to me that I must offer them as much choice as I possibly could, as much as I could imagine for myself, and then see what happened. These young East Enders were being offered an ideological menu that was only dulling all their palates.

Management committee meetings at Kingsley Hall became increasing fraught occasions. Three years in, Susan, a wise and balanced local mum, who was now the Chair of the organization (the title 'Chairman' was definitely not allowed) was increasingly exasperated with the political games that were being played out there. At one meeting a member of the local Marxist group suggested that, while the centre should be open to all the community, it should ban the police, any religious people or anyone, for that matter, who was not a member of the Labour Party. I asked who that would actually leave free to walk across the threshold. These people said they were concerned about humanitarian issues, but many of them demonstrated an intense *dislike* of people – particularly people who did not share their own beliefs. We were creating a logic that held everyone responsible for everything, but which found no one actually taking responsibility for anything. All decisions were being reduced to the lowest common denominator. We were arguing endlessly about equal opportunities policies and yet the organization became unhappier by the day.

Like many other parts of the voluntary sector that I had come into contact with in east London, our organization mirrored the thinking and culture of the public sector. It had forgotten who it was there to serve. All it knew for certain was that it was against anything that reeked of enterprise and entrepreneurship. During one memorable meeting, I suggested that it might be sensible to employ a director.

I was immediately attacked by every single other person in the room. These early decisions would set a tone that would paralyse the organization for more than twenty years.

Lylie could see what was happening and she despaired. Liberal ideology was running amuck and no one seemed to be able to stop it. It seemed to have a life of its own. People talked about their 'rights' but rarely about their 'responsibilities'. The local community was suffering as a consequence. Doris and Muriel Lester would have despaired.

The voluntary sector talks a lot today about the importance of their values, as though there is a logical and inevitable link between virtuous motives and the consequences they produce. Governments often assume the same uncritical stance. Kingsley Hall was teaching me that motives and consequences are very different things and, in fact, at times they might not have anything in common at all. You can hold all the right values and purest motives in the world as an organization, but the consequences of your actions could, as a matter of fact, be a disaster for the people you're there to serve. On the other hand, an organization can hold values and motives that seem to be dubious but which, ironically, can trigger consequences that have a very positive effect on people. This is a lesson, the law of unintended consequences, that New Labour would do well to learn.

The human cost of all of this political infighting became clear to me when we were asked to host a visit by Lord Fenner Brockway, the editor of the *Labour Leader*, the official organ of the Independent Labour Party. He had been an active campaigner against the First World War and secretary of the No Conscription Fellowship. He had been court-martialled at Chester and imprisoned at Wormwood Scrubs, Wandsworth and Lincoln in 1919. He was also one of the founders of CND. Now well into his nineties, Fenner had been invited to speak at a CND rally which was to be held in the Kingsley Hall building.

He arrived one cold Sunday afternoon with the Indian High Commissioner in tow, who was very interested to see the building where Gandhi had stayed. Due to our democratic paralysis, nobody could take charge and lead the committee, which in turn meant that no one welcomed Fenner to Kingsley Hall properly. Both he and the High Commissioner drifted through the buildings like lost sheep. They were both deeply confused, and no doubt a little offended, by the apparent lack of hospitality extended to them. The whole visit was a shambles from beginning to end. We had wasted an important opportunity by offering no sense of welcome or clarity of purpose. We were an ideological mess, and this one event was only a sign of things to come.

In January 1985, in the midst of these shenanigans, the building works were finished and we had to organize the opening celebrations. It had been suggested that Sir Richard Attenborough, who had visited Kingsley Hall when filming his award-winning epic life of Gandhi, should be asked to open the buildings along with Lylie, and that we should organize a firework and laser show from the roof to crown off the evening. Countless difficult meetings followed and, against all the 'democratic' principles and wholly due to pressure of time, I was asked to take responsibility for this part of the proceedings. I was to organize a twenty-minute firework display which would, possibly for the first time ever in east London, include a laser show. All of which would be set to music by Michael Jackson, Queen and the London Symphony Orchestra.

The night before the event two health and safety officers arrived from Tower Hamlets Council and the GLC. The local company I had booked to run the event, on the recommendation of one of the management committee, included an expert in the science of lasers who turned out to be rather less competent than I'd been led to believe. One of this man's first mistakes was to demonstrate to the health and safety officers the wonders of this new technology, which included a large water pipe, which ran from the large laser amplifier plugged into the mains electricity, to the water tap. The 'expert' explained in great detail how much heat and energy this infernal machine produced once it was switched on and he would, he said, demonstrate his point by lighting a cigarette from the intense green light emanating from within the open machine just a small distance away. As he took out the cigarette, it started to rain; and as he bent low over the machine to breathe in the light with the tip of the cigarette, his long hair smothered the rest of the open circuits.

The two health and safety officers could barely control themselves and immediately asked that the machine be switched off. Twenty-four hours to go before the great man arrived and we had a crisis. I took the officers downstairs, made some tea and encouraged the 'expert' to find a way to protect the exposed equipment from the rain. An hour and half later, after a detailed discussion about what the two officers would and would not allow to happen, we returned to the roof. The expert had at last found a solution to what was now a very wet evening. Ingeniously, brilliantly, he had placing an old fifties deckchair over the amplifier to protect it from the rain.

We had a lot more negotiating to do!

Eventually, when we had at last complied with their demands, I agreed that the officers could both stand next to the equipment and keep watch over the expert during the proceedings and if at any time during the light show they were unhappy with what they saw, they had my permission to switch the infernal machine off. They agreed.

I kept all of this negotiation at a distance from the management committee just in case.

The day arrived and so did Sir Richard Attenborough, pulling up in his bright green Rolls Royce. I opened the car door and led him and his wife, through the crowds that had gathered, on to the raised stage outside the front doors of the hall. Richard had prepared a speech, I had prepared a microphone and he began to speak. Standing just to his left I could see some young East End boys up for a laugh. One of them had a piece of chocolate cake, which he had taken from the bunfight the local people had been invited to join in with an hour before the finale. Just as Richard began to get into his stride, this young man decided to launch a piece of his chocolate cake at him. It was a perfect shot, and hit him square on his glasses, which he then had to remove. The audience and stage party froze.

Suddenly a bold and authoritative voice at the side of me, in the form of his wife, the actress Sylvia Syms, boomed out: 'On with the show, darling.' And, like the trouper he is, he put the written speech down and enthused us all with a marvellous ad-libbed speech. I have a picture of the unfortunate event, and will hold it dear as a keepsake for ever.

The firework and laser show turned out to be a considerable success. Richard told me that he had only ever seen anything like it at the Michael Jackson concert he had recently attended in New York. I was well pleased. The neighbours, however, in the twenty-five-storey tower blocks at the end of Bruce Road, whose windows faced west, were not. They could not see the fireworks and were sure that the very loud explosions that they could hear outside were, in fact, an IRA terrorist attack. They rang the police.

# creating change: a lifetime's task

**S**ir Richard Attenborough was now offering to put more money into the project, totally unaware of the desperate state of the organization. Kingsley Hall was drowning in half-baked political correctness. We were asking him to put money towards what was fast becoming, and would remain for over twenty years, a sinking ship.

Because of its links with Gandhi, Kingsley Hall had attracted all sorts of people who wanted to hitch their wagon to his. I soon came to realize that many of them had a sentimental image of the great man. One such group was the Gandhi Foundation. As a good liberal I initially gave them time and encouraged their work. However, it soon became clear that they were a group of very nice people who not only had a romantic view of Gandhi but also of the East End of London. Lylie kept me grounded in all of this. Gandhi had frequently been accused of changing his mind on important subjects. He was an openly creative thinker who was not burdened with a fundamentalist spirit. He was in touch with the world around him at a deep level and understood, like an artist or an entrepreneur, how to make it pliable and bring change. Life, for him, Lylie reminded me, was a creative process. He was an opportunist and knew instinctively how to take something as simple as salt and use it to turn India against the British.

Muriel Lester said in her book, *It Occurred to Me*, that you only become part of a place when you rest your head there. Gandhi, it seemed clear to me, would have moved in and would have taken responsibility for the consequences of his actions. The Gandhi Foundation epitomized too much modern thinking, which believes you can change the world through a policy paper at little personal cost. Gandhi knew you couldn't, so did Muriel and Doris.

Real change is not a soft option: it is costly and does not come easy. It demands real personal sacrifice. It requires a lifetime commitment, not a government cycle. These newcomers would be blown away at the first sign of trouble, yet they symbolized so much of the response to the modern world of the liberal elite.

My time with Kingsley Hall was frustrating and wearying. It unsettled me and somewhere deep down it strengthened my resolve to challenge the internal logic that underpinned it and which, I knew, represented the inner logic of many schools, health centres and other parts of the public sector. It was built on theories about equality and race, and it championed the virtue of endless meetings. It had no real foundation in an understanding of what it means to be a human being. It took a man called Santiago to bring me to my senses and put these feelings of frustration into positive, and inspiring, perspective.

# coming home

Santiago Bell arrived at my vestry door one Tuesday afternoon in 1985. A few weeks earlier I had been travelling to Birmingham with a journalist. I had been invited to speak at a conference organized by Christian Aid and Oxfam about my recent trip to El Salvador and Nicaragua. During the car journey, the journalist told me that she had a very talented Chilean exile doing some work for her at the moment, putting up shelves in her house, and that he was looking for a place to build himself a workshop. I told her that I had lots of empty rooms at the church and that I was sure I could help.

The man I saw when I opened the door that day, with his weathered face and wise eyes, had manifestly been through a terrible ordeal. I invited him in and we sat down and talked for hours. In broken English, Santiago told me of his life. He had been a state governor in his home country before 1973 when Augusto Pinochet orchestrated the coup d'état that deposed President Allende, with whom Santiago had strong links. He had been arrested almost immediately and spent many months incarcerated in a Chilean prison. On his release he had been allowed to come to Britain because his grandfather was Scottish and therefore he had a British passport. As we talked, I found out that he was a good friend of the famous Latin American educationalist Paulo Freire, and that he and his wife Miriam had adopted street children into their home. He was looking for somewhere to rebuild his life in a new country. Everything in my being told me that that place was right here, with me, in Bromley-by-Bow.

The church had no money at the time. Our only assets when I arrived were twelve elderly people, a suite of rundown church buildings and £400 in the bank. I could offer him very, very little except my derelict empty room next to the 'rifle room'. This did not worry Santiago: he could build something out of nothing. He set to work.

He began to arrive each day with pieces of timber he had scavenged from local skips. He soon cleared the room, painted the walls white, brought in a few personal tools and began to build – or, more accurately, sculpt – a workbench. The joints were so close fitting, and it was all so expertly made, that it could have taken the weight of an elephant. This was no ordinary joiner and Su knew it. The gossip began to get around. Two likely lads making furniture for Janet Street-Porter's house on the Isle of Dogs arrived, asking for Santiago's advice. Ethel introduced herself and was graciously welcomed into his workshop – which was fast becoming his home. Tools were carefully placed in handmade racks on the walls like works of art, and every afternoon after my piano practice I would stop by for a chat.

Day by day, story by story, I began to understand what he had been through. I heard about the horrific events that he both endured and witnessed in prison. How he had become one of the many nameless individuals in Chile who had 'disappeared', and how Miriam and their many children had thought him dead for six months. I was told how, in order to keep sane in a small prison cell, he had performed the priestly function of taking bread and water each day at a set time, sharing it as a Eucharist with his cellmates. He was being brutalized daily, and knew full well that death was an ever-present reality.

What he said about creating a sense of order in the middle of an unpredictable and terrifying reality really hit home. He had rules for coping with the insanity of it all: keep the rhythm, keep the pace, turn a 'nowhere' into 'somewhere'. Create something out of nothing, create order out of chaos. During those afternoons, and what turned into countless years, of conversations with Santiago, I came to know a sensitive artist, a truly great sculptor and a wise man who knew much about the world and the ways of human beings. He was fast becoming a father figure to Su. He also knew and understood how to build a community. He knew that real change must be built of something solid, built timber by timber, relationship by relationship. Community was not about talk but about action, doing things together.

Santiago brought with him an understanding of human community whose roots ran deep within Latin American Catholicism and the Judaeo-Christian traditions. It was a way of thinking that was profoundly at odds with modern ideas about change, a gentle, often contradictory, but strangely resilient way of seeing human life, which could look evil in the eye and take it on. This way of living could survive on the streets of Bosnia, Iraq and Zimbabwe. It had been forged in the fires of adversity. It was absolutely attentive to the detail of life.

Contradictory and challenging as Santiago was, I felt his

approach to life somehow fitted with my own endeavours in Bromley-by-Bow. His way of living and of understanding the world was born out of adversity and depended on building deeply resilient human connections and being absolutely attentive to the detail of life. I was building a team, forging strong relationships, setting out on a journey, constantly retelling and rehearsing my story with no business plan, unsure what each day would bring. I knew it would require a creative and flexible spirit to spot opportunities, and great persistence and clarity of purpose to stay the course. I had to be very careful to keep a steady pace, create order, one step at a time. Santiago knew how to do just that: he was giving me the tools for survival. Santiago had not a clue about money, yet in those early months he had attracted a wide range of local creative people and artists to the church buildings. Slowly and surely, we were beginning to operate like a real team.

Together, we started to build what was to become the Bromley-by-Bow Centre, a laboratory for social innovation and enterprise. This would not be another community centre – a tacky, rundown public-sector building with posters on the wall – but a 'centre of community and entrepreneurship' defined by innovative design, a welcoming environment and quality furnishings, with hard work, enterprise and creativity at its heart, not ideology and theory. Santiago had taught me that there was an organic way to build a project which was based on a network of relationships, and which had the potential to grow exponentially. It would develop some of the thinking that surrounded Muriel and Doris Lester's work at Kingsley Hall but not follow it blindly. Today the Bromley-by-Bow Centre employs over a hundred staff, and runs over 100 activities each week in high-quality buildings purposely designed. It has transformed the derelict three-acre recreation ground which surrounds our buildings into a beautiful, award-winning community park. It has helped to establish a £300 million local housing company which now manages over eight thousand properties across Poplar. It has become a catalyst demonstrating practical social innovation and change, and has made an impact not just locally but nationally and internationally as well. Now the Centre finds itself situated directly across the road from the 2012 Olympic site, and indeed we played an important part in encouraging the Olympics to come to the Lower Lea Valley.

Santiago's recent funeral was a torturously emotional affair in which grandchildren and countless family members were called upon to speak, through their tears, about his life. Those of us who had come to know him while he had been here in Britain looked on. As the large, handmade, plane wood coffin disappeared into the fires, we were all dramatically called to attention by his Latin American *compadres*. Loudly and with great abandon their words rang out across the City of London cemetery chapel: 'Santiago Bell *presente*! Santiago Bell *presente*! Santiago Bell *presente*!' He would have loved it. The revolutionary who did not believe in the bullet and the gun but in the power of human love was dead, but his thoughts were still alive in all who were present.

Santiago taught me about turning dreams into reality – he taught me how that yearning has a dynamic to it that is incredibly powerful. It is important, simply, to be open and alive to possibility, to encourage people rather than to be suspicious of them, and to see the potential for success rather than the potential for failure. This is where true knowledge and learning can be found, much more so than in an arid policy paper, which can simply not hope to capture the power there is to be found in a human being.

# dancing with dinosaurs

ower Hamlets had a new Liberal Democrat council at the time. In a bid to bring decision-making closer to the community, the Lib Dems had divided the borough into seven neighbourhoods which would have some semblance of devolved control over the decisions that affected them. It sounded like an interesting idea. We later came to realize that the fundamental concerns behind this thinking were wrong – this approach, in common with the approaches of other parties which would follow, cared more about implementing structures than about working with local leaders and the agents of change. The frequently shifting political landscape was tough on the people of Bow. It seemed that every change was followed by at least three years of chaos while new 'structures' were implemented and old ones taken down. Amid a lot of talk about structure and process, very little seemed to be achieved for the community in any kind of practical way. A great deal of public money was spent on new public-sector buildings and infrastructure and yet there was never really time for it all to settle down before the next political cycle and the Lib Dems lost power. It was frustrating and, from my point of view and the point of view of the people I was working with, it was becoming harder and harder to accept that this kind of 'democracy' was worth a hill of beans.

During these chaotic years, my team and I decided to forge ahead, very much in spite of local politicking: we would attempt to get people from the voluntary sector working together with people from the public sector on a joint project which could, we hoped, offer an intelligent response to some of the so-called intractable social problems we were all aware of.

Along with Bill Tomlinson, then the local chief executive in our neighbourhood, we decided to look at each area of council activity and see which services could be contracted out to the Bromley-by-Bow Centre – we were proposing a long-term contractual relationship, rather than one based on short-term grants. Every Friday afternoon, my colleagues Donald Findley and Allison Trimble sat down with Bill and one of the heads of services – community education or social services, for example – and attempted to come to an agreement that would move the project forward. Some of the conversations were positive; some were straightforwardly hostile; but eventually we agreed a contract comprising three elements of responsibility:

1. Running community education classes
2. Providing care services for local elderly and disabled people
3. Running the local park

It was just about possible for the slimmed-down local authority of Poplar to negotiate with just one community organization to work out the practical – legal and financial –

ramifications of entering into a contractual relationship. If the process had been opened up to all local voluntary-sector organizations (if it would have been strictly democratic and concerned with being 'fair') it would most likely have become little more than a talking shop. This may well be why good examples of imaginative contracting are still so rare.

One week after the ink was dry, the Liberal Democrats finally lost control of the borough to New Labour – though our ward remained Liberal. As usual, structures had to change. The infrastructure of the seven neighbourhoods was swiftly removed and in its place Labour invented seven committees, which would run the borough instead. It frankly seemed like a joke – but nobody was laughing. And, what was more, our first serious attempt at engaging with the public sector seemed to be dead in the water.

For two years there was little point trying to negotiate with the new administration, which saw us as part of the Liberal 'old guard'. The fact that we were an independent organization with no political affiliation whatsoever didn't seem to matter. Any further attempts to develop a coherent range of health, care and education services delivered by local people for local people were thwarted – and I began to feel that the main reason for this was that we lacked an individual within the political system who was prepared to invest the time, and cared enough about the project, to get the details right. Those people who could have helped us obviously – and, I might say, reasonably – had other priorities. We would have to bide our time until that person came along.

It was not until early in 2000 that a more dynamic

relationship began to develop between the Centre and the Council and indeed the Health Service. It was made possible because new, more business-minded leadership teams were thankfully to appear in these public-sector bodies. In 2005 we began to work more closely with Christine Gilbert, the new Chief Executive of Tower Hamlets Council (now head of Ofsted). The Centre was also deepening its partnerships with Poplar Harca, the housing company I had helped establish, and Leaside Regeneration Ltd, which manages a £100 million regeneration programme in the area surrounding Bromley-by-Bow and of which I was a founding director. Working in partnership, we all wanted to scale up our work and transcend the New Labour hype about 'joined-up thinking', 'partnership with the voluntary sector' and 'social enterprise' – we wanted to achieve the practical results which these fine words and attractive sound bites seemed to promise but which few in either the voluntary or public sectors were experienced enough to know how to deliver. It was clear to me that much policy thinking about 'joined-up working' was passing into the public sector but few of the officers in these organizations had the faintest clue how to turn these ideas into desired practice. They were facing the same problem my son faced with the Noddy jigsaw. We felt that our task was to demonstrate real 'joined-up working', partnership in practice.

I began by arranging an informal dinner at the Bromley-by-Bow Centre. This first meeting helped us to develop a clearer understanding of each other's agendas and the different anxieties we all faced. As it turned out, we actually had more in common than many of us had suspected. We needed to move beyond our worries and suspicions to build a more trusting relationship if we were really going to work as a team. Very gradually in the following months, as trust and understanding between us strengthened and we began to 'learn by doing' projects together, we formed a closer working partnership. Christine invited me to speak to her senior management team at the council and I pointed out to them the practical result of this partnership: within eight months from our conception to operation, we had together delivered to the people of Tower Hamlets a stunning new business centre, which we built in the park behind our buildings. Not any old business centre either, but a piece of quality design by the architect Gordon MacLaren constructed using fine oak topped with a striking grass-covered roof. Within two years the centre had incubated seventeen brand-new social businesses across the borough. By working together, we had not only delivered a piece of first-class design which would raise both the profile and aspirations of the area, but we had delivered it on time and on cost, and we had a building which today provides business support to twenty-three social enterprises, each one in turn making working connections with other projects across the borough.

Some government ministers and public-sector officials worry about how fair it would be to give their full backing to the social entrepreneurial approach. They believe that the entire voluntary sector should be treated equally, regardless; that fairness demands such a response. When I think of this, I think of something my friend the Reverend Peter Thomson once told me. Peter is a pioneer of the social entrepreneurial approach, whose work goes back to the 1960s. He is also one of Tony Blair's closest friends and clearly an important influence during his formation of the New Labour agenda. Peter was entirely unmoved by this idea of 'fairness'. His response to it was to turn it on its head and ask, 'But whom are you being fair *to*?' From this perspective, it quickly becomes clear that government has to make a choice between being 'fair' to the voluntary sector and being 'fair' to the people on Britain's estates.

My colleague Professor Paul Brickell, who now runs Leaside Regeneration and was formerly CEO at Bromley-by-Bow, once told me of his experience of funding when, during his early career as a scientist, he ran one of the genetics laboratories at Great Ormond Street Children's Hospital. When funders there were deciding which research to invest their money in, they did not follow the logic of the public and charitable sectors. They didn't worry about being fair to all of the scientists who were researching in the field of childhood cancer, for example. Instead, they chose to put what money they had available to them behind the very best research, the very best scientists and doctors, regardless of how it might look to colleagues. They were very clear about whom they needed to be fair to – not the scientific community at large, but the patients who required the best and most promising treatments on offer.

Both New Labour and the Conservative Party seem quite confused about this whole area. Few have understood that fairness actually demands that you back success: you put your trust in people who can demonstrate to you that they can get results. You back experience, and get behind those individuals and their teams who over many years have come to understand the detail of their subject and are now capable of delivering results – something business has long understood. Such an approach, I would argue, is actually far fairer in the long term to the residents in the estates in Bromley-by-Bow, for example. It will use taxpayers' money far more efficiently. There is nothing wrong with being a beginner in the charity business, but to pretend that someone who started yesterday is on the same level as someone who has been delivering successful outcomes for over twenty years is ludicrous, not to say dangerous and profoundly *unfair*.

This is an uncomfortable issue, but I believe it really must be faced up to, and quickly: millions of pounds of public monies are being wasted as a result of the lack of clarity this thinking encourages. A responsible society has to decide which stones to roll with – do we back the stones that have forward momentum, or do we make them all just a little more square just in case one tries to move faster than the others? If we don't back success, the result will be a culture – and a society – of failure and mediocrity.

# people before structures

Bow was once famous for its pottery – a quick browse on eBay will show that well-preserved pieces of Bow porcelain are highly sought-after these days. We thought it would be fantastic to rekindle the pottery tradition at the Centre, bring it back to the heart of Bromley-by-Bow. But we had no potter. And we had no kiln. All we had was an empty room that I had set aside, in hope.

My first move was to put an advert up outside the church:

KILN WANTED. ENQUIRE WITHIN.

It had become my habit to leave the doors to the church building open, so that passers-by knew there was life inside and that we were not closed to them. I was desperate to bring the outside in, to encourage contact with the people I was there for. Opening up one day, I watched as a young dark-haired woman, out walking her dog, stopped to read my advert. The dog was tethered to a piece of string. They both looked up at me.

'Are you looking for a kiln, then?' she asked, with a nervous grin.

'Yes, I am indeed,' I replied, sensing a bite. 'Why, do you have one?'

'Funnily enough, I do. It's never been used. It's in our house, just down the street there. Why don't you come over for a cup of tea?'

It was an offer I couldn't possibly refuse.

Most of the pre-war two-up-two-down housing which had been built in our part of the East End had been bombed out of existence during the Blitz, but one row of terraces survived just down the road, an obstinate reminder of past times. These houses were in poor condition. The GLC had moved all of the former residents out into local flats and tenements, with a view to demolishing them. However, this hadn't come to pass and, over the years, they had come to be occupied in the main by a bunch of artists looking for a cheap place in London – among them this young woman, whose name I now knew to be Margy, her husband, Frank, and their two children, Theo and Nicky.

When I eventually went to meet her I was greeted by Theo, dressed in a bright blue cape and with a superhero arm thrust out in front of him, dashing with the kind of energy only a young boy can muster through the largely empty rooms. They'd moved in with just £5 worth of furniture. I could smell oil paint.

This young hero would eventually gain a place at Cambridge to study architecture, and end up working for the Eden Project in Cornwall. But for now he was saving the world in other ways. Back then, I had no idea what effect a lifetime spent in Bromley-by-Bow might have on his future. I was just there to buy a kiln.

Margy and I sat down and began to get acquainted. She

had grown up in Africa and her early life had been a peripatetic one, moving from place to place with her sisters. She had eventually struck out on her own to come to London and study art. She'd been living in a squat which was masquerading as a fire station when she met and fell in love with Frank.

Margy was a fine artist. Somewhere along the way, she had acquired a kiln. We finished the tea.

'I want to buy the kiln from you, Margy. And I want you to teach a pottery class. What d'you think?'

I later discovered that she had never taught pottery in her life, but she agreed to my suggestion without hesitation. She liked the idea, and would have a go. It was a spirit I learnt to love, and her whole family shared the same easygoing, can-do attitude – they became a sounding board for me for years to come.

# we are the environments
# we live in

I continued to take the service every Sunday for the same twelve elderly people who'd greeted me that very first day. But I wanted to serve the church by engaging in a practical way with the local neighbourhood. The church was losing serious ground in areas such as this, and I was determined that I would do things differently to try to reverse that trend.

As I stood by the church door looking in one day, I had something of a revelation: this place, dilapidated as it still was, looked more like a lecture theatre than a community space. The whole set-up – pulpit up front, for me to proclaim from on high; the pews lined up in strict, formal, meek lines before it. There was a deliberate separation between church and congregation in the very architecture, and I found myself thinking that it was no wonder people weren't particularly attracted to drop in on their way back from Tesco or taking the kids to school. Nothing here looked comforting, attractive or supportive. The message seemed to be: I will talk and you will listen. Where was the sense of sharing and community in that?

The East End had sustained a lot of bombing during the Blitz, and only the 120-year-old church hall of the original building had survived. Renovations during the fifties were largely uninspiring and certainly did not seem to anticipate that the area would change substantially. In fact, the area had changed a great deal post-war, in large part due to the winding down of work at the docks. People were bettering themselves and moving away, to new estates in Dagenham and Essex. Southend was the ultimate dream destination for an East Ender intent on success. In their place settled a large immigrant population (the East End had a long history of immigration, which found its stride during the post-war years).

To illustrate the way in which the building itself was poorly designed to serve the community, I only had to recall the first funeral I had been called upon to conduct. It had been an excruciating affair. The entrance foyer resembled entrance foyers of countless churches up and down the country – only in this case the builder had miscalculated the dimensions. I realized this to my horror when, before the service, the pall-bearers could not negotiate the right and left turns through the two doors in the lobby without being forced to upend the coffin. This appalling mistake was bad enough, but the solution the powers that be came up with only added insult to injury: a sliding glass window in the foyer wall, through which the coffin could be passed. I was horrified – it was like some kind of fast-food serving hatch, embarrassing for me and profoundly disturbing for the mourners.

I began to walk through the buildings, facing up to reality. They were awkward and littered with cheap tarnished brass plaques to tell you that the flower vase was placed in memory of Sid Piper's wife and so forth. It felt like I was walking through a cold, grey mausoleum, some vault from a bygone era. I had to change this place, and quickly.

My first move was to get down from the pulpit. With Santiago's help, I redesigned the church so that it was in the round, to encourage a feeling of sharing and to break down some outdated boundaries. We strung a ring of twelve candles up above the communion table and brought in a fan heater to warm up the room while we worked on fixing the central heating. It was immediately more welcoming.

I was soon called on to perform my first baptism. Dave and Anne were proud new East End parents of a daughter, Sarah. They all lived on the sixth floor of one of the two rundown tower blocks across the road from the church. Their living room faced out onto the busy Blackwall Tunnel approach road. They had no double glazing. When I went to pay them a visit about the baptism, I wanted to discover how this event might become a celebration not only of Sarah's life but also of their life together: a celebration of the whole family. I wanted to remind them that the baptism was not a private matter in a privatizing culture – it took place in a public building to remind us that Sarah was a part of the community. Finally, I proposed a deal: this would be a two-way agreement. I would baptize their daughter, but in exchange I wanted them to come back each year, on the anniversary, to light the baptism candle and share tea and cakes with us. We shook hands. This became a ritual which would, in time, involve ever greater numbers of people.

I had a sense that building up a sense of community in an area where so many people were isolated would mean creating some kind of rhythm around which they could orientate themselves. I understood that all the strategizing and report-writing about the problems of the inner city, or the failure of the church in urban areas, were failing because they didn't engage with the people themselves. Where they saw failure, I realized there was great potential – and it was there all along, in the very people who walked up and down the streets. My task was to begin a conversation: as simple, and as difficult, as that. This community would flourish only if the people in it began talking to each other and taking more personal responsibility together for the area in which they lived.

Mary was interested in starting an organization that would help to improve the lives of disabled people who lived in the area. She was disabled herself. She already had a name: 'Out and About'. In Bromley-by-Bow there were a lot of disabled people, many of them living in tower blocks – often quite literally trapped there because of lack of attention to disabled access – and more or less forgotten about. Mary felt passionately about wanting to challenge this apathy within the community and create an integrated response. But she had next to no money in her charitable account. When she came to discuss it with me, I could see both that there was a demand for the service she was proposing and that she was the right person to make it work if she had the resources to do so. We struck an agreement – we would work together as partners. I would rent her a space in the building, and in return she would work with me to integrate the project into the community I was trying to establish.

Our first task, prosaic enough, was tackling the toilets. Up until then, I had managed with just one gents' and one ladies'. Incredibly, there had been no disabled facility. Mary and I were determined that no matter what people thought of the rest of the place, they would be impressed by the loos! It was marble all the way, as far as we were concerned. Impressed by her resolve, I agreed to the expensive fittings she happily proposed: thinking big and bold, having ambition, was what this whole venture was about, and, as far as I was concerned, that applied to the loos as much as it did to everything else. It certainly got people's tongues wagging.

There was the minor matter of raising the £5000 it was going to cost. This was my first attempt at honing my skills in fundraising. Mary and I began to make our approaches and, though we had to learn as we went along, it turned out I was good at inspiring potential funders with a vision of what we wanted to achieve, while Mary had a knack for ensuring our applications were filled in properly and handed in on time. Eventually we raised the money we needed. The resulting toilets looked great, of course, and they have stood the test of time even twenty-one years down the line. In a funny way, they epitomized my view of the endeavour – which was that we should never be confined in our thinking, and that we should demand quality from the places we live.

The environments we live, work and play in profoundly affect how we are as human beings and how we relate to each other. I learned this from Bromley-by-Bow. It was such a dump down there when I first arrived. We were determined to create a really nice space. As I began to deliver this, I realized that people took it as a sign of respect for themselves and their children – they felt they were being taken seriously. When we are careful about the way we create a physical environment, when we pay attention to every detail of it, people start to think about themselves and each other differently. What was becoming clear was how value judgements about Bromley-by-Bow had been keeping it down all these years: when we later wrote to English Partnerships, a government body, outlining our plans to build a top-quality restaurant with granite work surfaces and limestone flooring on our site, we received a response telling us that this was far too high quality for such a rundown area. It demonstrated an extraordinarily skewed logic and a total lack of even a fundamental understanding of the human spirit. I was treating people as people; they were treating people as statistics. If you give people quality, if you treat them with respect, they will respond in kind. A café that offers people instant coffee in a foam cup gives a very different message from a café that offers them a range of coffee in elegant cups which are nice to drink from – it might sound silly, but at the time all the people in my area had on offer was instant coffee, literally and metaphorically. It was all they were deemed worthy of. Businesses under-stand that they need to take care over details and quality, because they face their customers. What was clear from my time in Bromley-by-Bow was that the housing associations, regeneration bodies, voluntary sector and other bodies in the area wanting to 'make a difference' were all facing towards government – they had to, because they were dependent on government funding. However, this meant that their view of reality would profoundly differ from that of their customers, local residents, for whom the whims and concerns of such things as government funding bodies were of absolutely no concern.

There was a real disconnection at this time on the estates in my area. People lived in their own little worlds. It had become 'right on' to live in the East End – it was trendy with a kind of liberal, artistic bunch – which was fantastic to see, but it was disappointing to realize that few of these really talented people actually knew their working-class neighbours. Their backgrounds were in university and art colleges, they came from the suburbs, and they by and large shared a view that socialism was 'good' and business was 'bad'. My observation, though, had been that politicians of all colours – red, blue, green, yellow, you name it, socialism included (though it was a kind of heresy to say it at the time) – had failed the people of the borough of Tower Hamlets.

Lorca arrived blissfully unaware of all of the social turmoil I was determined to battle. She was an artist, a sculptor who carved stone, and all she wanted was a place to make into a studio so that she could get on with her work. She heard about me on the grapevine via the small army of artists who lived in the area, and eventually came to see what all the fuss was about. I liked her a lot, and agreed that she could have the damp yard at the back of the buildings. With Santiago's help she began to develop an outdoor studio. She had real skill and sensitivity, and she put a lot of time into helping to strengthen the links between the Centre and the artistic community.

When we began to think about further renovations to the church, she offered to carve two angels, which would hang over the new doorway, as if in mid-flight, and announce our presence to the world. Su was the inspiration for one of these cherubic carvings; the other was made in the likeness of Malachi, a Rastafarian string sandal maker who had joined the team around this time. Su's classical golden locks and Malachi's long dreads made quite an impression, and definitely raised a smile!

Three years had passed, and I was beginning to understand that the small things really mattered. One of my favourite phrases today is 'the devil is in the detail' because in everything we do at Bromley-by-Bow, and in everything the people around me at the time were doing, there was a great amount of purpose about and pride taken in even the most minute details of life.

# the mind's the standard
# of the man

Encouraged by our initial success, Mary went on to raise money to build a resource centre for the disabled. It was named after Joseph Merrick, the Elephant Man, whose remains were still to be found just down the road from us, in the London Hospital in Whitechapel. For the opening ceremony, Santiago carved a plaque and engraved it with words from a hymn Joseph Merrick had been fond of:

> 'Tis true, my form is something odd
> but blaming me, is blaming God,
> Could I create myself anew?
> I would not fail in pleasing you.
>
> If I could reach from pole to pole
> Or grasp the ocean with a span,
> I would be measured by the soul
> The Mind's the standard of the Man.
>
> 'False Greatness', Isaac Watts

One of the most severely disabled people at the Centre was Colin. Every morning at 9 a.m., as regular as clockwork,

I would open up and see, at a distance, Colin's dark blue Ford Escort approaching down the street. I would watch then as the car transformed: a door would open, followed by a piece of machinery which would slowly eject from behind the driver's seat. Attached to this would be a folded-up wheelchair. Colin would then contort his inflexible body, disconnect the chair from the contraption that delivered it from the car to the pavement, and proceed to do battle with it until it was fully open and ready for action. Another button was pressed and the driver's seat would swing out at ninety degrees, revealing Colin to the world at large to hang, suspended, over the pavement. Finally, Colin would haul himself into the wheelchair. The whole palaver took about fifteen minutes. And this was before he'd locked the car and begun his journey into the building.

Very little of Colin's body worked apart from his neck, which allowed twenty degrees of movement from side to side. In spite of this, he had educated himself, taught himself to drive, managed to find a specially adapted car so that he could be mobile, and work a full-time job at the Centre. People like Colin and Mary were really inspiring for us – they both believed in a cause and were not interested in people's sympathy or well-meaning words. They simply wanted to work with people who could help deliver results. I learned a lot from them.

# the devil is in the detail

**E**arly on, after the success with Su and the boat, we agreed that one strategy we would employ was to say 'yes' to everyone who wanted to use our largely rundown buildings. It would have been easy to find reasons to say 'no', as is usual with many charitable and social organizations. But that approach didn't seem to work for anyone – it simply discouraged creativity and enterprise. We decided to give our space over to the community and see what happened – it could certainly be no worse. As Jenny was to put it many years later, 'When Andrew came in 1984 we decided to throw our knickers over the garden fence. What had we to lose?' (Ethel's twinkle-eyed response to which was, 'Oooh, Jenny, what are you saying?')

Getting real about your assets when you're facing a time of crisis is crucial. I had a mere £400 in the bank. I knew that the people I met were generous with the little they had. Their generosity of spirit was forged out of a lot of hardship. I was encouraged to follow suit. These people were not for running away from the truth of a situation – they were prepared to get real. Many years later I thanked them for their straightforwardness in sticking to their early promises.

I was starting to put more form to the idea that marrying

the approach of the artist and the entrepreneur could be a lot more profitable than that of the policy-paper-wielding researcher, politician or charity worker. It was very clear to me that it was in forging relationships between people from different backgrounds that progress was to be made; in people being willing to 'learn by doing' and engage in practical activity together in an area over a long period of time – getting stuck into the detail – rather than focusing solely on rhetoric and long-winded debate.

Many years later, the businessman Paul Preston, who brought the McDonald's chain so successfully to Britain, told me how, in the very early days, he had focused on making a success out of just one McDonald's outlet, in Woolwich in South London. He had focused on apparently unimportant details such as where to source the milk they used and how to ensure it arrived on time each day; which chairs could withstand five hundred people each day dragging them across the floor; and how to find good-quality flooring which looks as good at the end of a day during which it has been trampled on by thousands of customers and mopped a hundred times as it did at the beginning. He understood that he must understand in great detail how to make one shop work successfully before he could successfully build thousands of shops.

In Bromley-by-Bow, my aim became to firmly nurture an entrepreneurial culture, in which people from all kinds of different backgrounds would work together to fashion their own futures. My hope was that, in working hard and creatively, and engaging with the messy details, we would build physical structures that actually worked in practice and that were run and used by people who believed in, and had an investment in, creating a successful, large-scale future. In staying with the aspirations, passions, hopes and fears of the people who live in 'forgotten' places, and helping them to take the raw material and talent they already have and use it in a truly creative new way, we would also build a team, build a common purpose: build a strong community.

# building a social business

n 1986, two years into the project at Bow, I was approached by Steve Goode and a group of local parents who had been trying to run a nursery in their small front room with twelve young children. It had all become too much and they were looking for bigger premises. The only space large enough to contain their needs was the church itself.

One dreary morning, I took a group of the parents to visit the church hall, somewhat dreading their reaction to the cold, sombre-looking space. To my surprise, their reaction was entirely positive. It was exactly what they were looking for.

'It's a little more complicated than you might think.' I told them. 'I use this hall for my church services every Sunday afternoon.'

'I bet you can't afford to pay for the upkeep and heating, though,' came the reply.

They had a point. I couldn't deny that it was a struggle.

'Why don't you move out,' one of the parents proposed, 'and we'll take over the running of the building?'

I had a better idea.

'Why don't we form a partnership?'

This was long before the idea of partnerships became trendy, but it seemed to me that we could all help each other out in this way. It wasn't long before I co-opted Su and Ethel in on the idea as well. What I proposed was this: we would rip out all the fixtures and fittings in the church, we would find an architect, and we would come up with a design which would allow us to use this space both as a church and as a nursery, the two existing in harmony, each unencumbered by the other.

We proposed to erect a canopy in the central space of the church, which could be raised and lowered by a rope-pulley system. This could be used to define a space which we hoped would be used for many different purposes: it would define a church big enough for a realistic congregation of forty people (much more realistic than the two hundred people that the previous premises had optimistically been designed for); it could be used as a theatre space; it would incorporate an art gallery, to exhibit works of art made locally – evidence of all the great talent and achievement in the area, on display in the very heart of this community, to counteract all the news we kept hearing about Bromley-by-Bow being an 'underachieving' and 'failing' area; and, of course, it would also be used as a nursery.

Around this canopied 'theatre of life' we proposed to build the first integrated nursery school in the UK, which would invite an intake both of the children of parents who needed help from Social Services or who were on the at-risk register, *and* of the children of professional parents – doctors, business people, lawyers – who could afford to pay for their child's place. We would develop a business plan and calculate the cost of each child's place. Mixing the

I moved to Bromley-by-Bow with my family in 1984, to become the minister in a little-used United Reformed Church on Bruce Road – in the very buildings which would, eventually, become the Bromley-by-Bow Centre.

This archway, which now forms the entrance to the Bromley-by-Bow Centre, originally belonged to Northumberland House, which stood near the Embankment. When that was pulled down, it was then used as the entrance to the garden of Tudor House. It was designed in the eighteenth century by William Kent, who also designed Holkham Hall, Chiswick House and Horse Guards.

Ethel (always in her grey woolly hat!) being given the key to our first minibus. She was one of twelve elderly people who attended the church service back in the early days. She had a great sense of humour and youthful spirit, and was always practical and supportive to me when the chips were down. We would eventually name a block of flats after her.

We redesigned the church so that it could be a multi-purpose area, bringing together an art gallery, a nursery (shown here), a toy library, a crèche and a performance space.

Santiago Bell was very important to me, a great inspiration and help in the early days. He was a master craftsman, and came to London after being imprisoned by Chilean dictator General Pinochet. Many of his beautiful carvings remain in the centre, and his memory is written into the fabric of the building.

The church and canopy, ready for worship.

This is probably what many people think Tower Hamlets looks like – the run-down, ugly council block, the burnt-out car.

Bob's Park – one of the original 'green lungs' of London, but by 1984 a derelict wasteland. Here we built a landscaped park, which in turn created a social enterprise – Green Dreams – with a turnover now in excess of £1 million.

Tessa Jowell (fifth from right) opened our new health centre in 1998. Zenith Rahman, a leader in the local Bengali community, is standing second from the right. This Healthy Living Centre was the first of its kind in the UK.

The park as it is today, with a view of the business centre, which was opened in 2005 and which now houses the Social Enterprise Hub. The Pie in the Sky café is to the right.

Me with Prince Charles on his first visit to the Bromley-by-Bow centre in 1995. He would prove to be a staunch supporter of our work. During his visit, he took a keen interest in the smallest details, and seemed to understand just how much they matter.

These plans, by our architect Gordon MacLaren, show our vision for the park. Many visitors describe it as an inspirational public space.

A personal note from Tony Blair in 1998 wishing us well with the launch of the Community Action Network, a national network for social entrepreneurs. In his first speech as Prime Minster in 1997, delivered on the Aylesbury estate, he said that New Labour would 'back thousands of social entrepreneurs'.

Meeting with Tony Blair in 1995 at The Great Banquet held at Banqueting House, Whitehall.

A mosaic designed by one of our resident artists, Sheenagh McKinlay, in the health centre courtyard where it can be enjoyed by everyone.

Twenty years on, the buildings that I took over are virtually unrecognizable. The Bromley-by-Bow Centre has been a true catalyst for change in an area that has, time and again, been dismissed as 'failing'.

children of paying parents with children supported by the state was unheard of at the time. The business model would ensure a careful balance of children from different social backgrounds and races, a nursery that would offer quality schooling for both rich and poor. I was keen for the school to be run like a social business (long before the term became popular), using clear business principles. So, just as if we were starting a small business, we developed a realistic business plan, asked our architect to create a model out of card and balsa wood of what we expected the final result to look like, and then approached potential backers.

Our first move was to invite Social Services to come and take a look at our proposal. Their representative was instantly sceptical. She had been working in child care for over twenty years, she told us. She had taken all of the courses and was well qualified, and she was here to tell us that it simply was not possible to have a place that could successfully function as a nursery, a crèche, an art gallery, a church and a space in which ceremonies as diverse as Eid and Passover could be celebrated. There were rules and regulations, didn't we know? To illustrate her point, she pulled out of her bag what seemed an encyclopaedic volume listing them all: a thousand reasons why nothing could be done, the final evidence in the case against our cause.

I looked around the table: the parents were fuming. Steve Goode, the leading light, looked bemused and so was I. We rose to her challenge. I pointed out that I was a Christian minister in the dissenting tradition of the church, from which social reformers like John Bunyan and Martin Luther King had been hewn and that, like them, my view was that when the rules governing a thing did not work then it was time to change them. And as I pointed out, the rules she was presenting me with today clearly had not worked in Bromley-by-Bow, which had not been transformed in any of the ways people had been promising it would over the last thirty years. The frost was turning into ice as we eyeballed each other. Eventually, she told me she would have to talk to her director. I was delighted! 'Get him down here, and let's meet him for ourselves.'

A fortnight later, the director arrived and, fortunately for us, he turned out to be one of the most entrepreneurially minded public servants that I had ever met. He spent a good deal of time considering the proposition. He began making suggestions, indicating a real sense of enthusiasm for our ideas, engaging with us and our vision with the kind of energy that I knew meant we had a supporter in our midst.

Steve Goode, whom I'd grown to like and trust more and more, and I began to work together closely to build the first high-quality integrated nursery in the UK. When we opened, Steve became the first nursery manager. Since then, the business has grown even further: Bow Childcare is now a stand-alone social enterprise working in partnership with the Bromley-by-Bow Centre, and running nurseries in Tower Hamlets, Newham and Hackney. In 2005 John Reid and Tessa Jowell joined us to open a new seventy-eight-place, quality integrated nursery just one hundred yards down the road from our first, built using the highest-quality materials. Hundreds of children, including my own, have attended our facilities and many local people have worked for us and gone on through the nursery to other things. None of this would have happened if we had not been strong willed in the face of initial opposition.

The experience with the nursery had been instructive. The professionals I had come into contact with were not bad people, but they had little or no entrepreneurial nous. They all seemed to come from similar academic backgrounds, and possessed very little practical entrepreneurial ability at all. Clearly they had not been offered the opportunity to develop these skills, or had not been encouraged to value, respect or find interest in entrepreneurship and business. Many of the courses that prepared students for work in the social sector seemed to be divorced from the realities about which their tutors lectured. I was unaware that many of the senior business people I was meeting around this time had clearly also come to similar conclusions. Britain's educational establishment was out of touch and failing not only the needs of British business but also the needs of the poor.

Theory works in common rooms and lecture halls, as a great way to open minds, spark debate and develop critical faculties. But take your theory down to the streets of east London and try to make any of it matter one bit in the context of the lives of the people you'll see there. Britain was in danger of producing a professional class of well-read and highly educated individuals who had no entrepreneurial skills or respect for business, and who did not know how to connect their ideas to daily, lived reality. They did not engage, like I did, in any meaningful way with people like Su or Ethel or the parents at the nursery – their concern was for policy, strategy, process and structure. The professionals seemed to me at the time to have erected a very high wall behind which they could hide and detach themselves from the ordinary realities and messy lives of east

Londoners – and therefore also from demands that might well be demanded of them personally.

The experience at the nursery has fed directly into the other ventures I've since been involved in. We do not follow political rhetoric but instead we follow tried and tested methods which have proved to work over many years of hard practical experience. We work in close-knit teams of people, not feuding representative committees, and we focus on a common goal and task. Working in this way we have seen the benefits of applying business logic and cultures to social goals – we are not philanthropists; we are not simply charities; we are social entrepreneurs connecting the logic of business to social need.

To my way of thinking – and, importantly, acting – the difference comes from getting to know people, understanding who the customer is, being prepared to be energetic on the ground, and being committed to seeing a venture work *in practice*. I believe it is time for an overhaul of government and the social sector – we need to start employing more people from entrepreneurial backgrounds to run things: because, quite simply, they have the experience. They know how to make stuff work.

# a human tragedy

Through our work at the Bromley-by-Bow Centre we were demonstrating innovative new ways of delivering public service. Our next big step was sparked by my experience, early on, with a young woman called Jean Vialls.

Jean was a volunteer in our Community Care project. She was thirty-five years old. She was struggling to care for her two children, aged sixteen and two. She also had to care for her elderly parents and support her brothers. And she had six months to live – Jean was dying from cancer. While her life slowly unravelled, it became clear that she was falling through the nets of statutory provision. As that happened it also became clear that her best friend and fellow volunteer in our Community Care project, Jackie, was becoming very important to Jean. Jackie was a local mum who quickly realized that Jean was not getting the support she deserved and needed from Social Services and the NHS. For months Jackie and my colleague Allison battled with the NHS and the other public services that were letting Jean and her family down. We kept a meticulously detailed record of our dealings on Jean's behalf.

The truth was that as Jean was dying it was her friends in our Community Care project that were caring for her, her children, her parents and her brothers. It was her extended family at the Bromley-by-Bow Centre that was providing the practical daily care that was required. And it was this regime of care by her friends and colleagues that made a difference in the final days of Jean's life. This was a lesson that would become embedded in the life of the Bromley-by-Bow Centre from that day on.

Six months after we met, I would conduct Jean's funeral.

Jean's story had become a matter for public debate and, soon after the funeral, the national press arrived on my doorstep. Three weeks later, I was invited to attend an inquiry into the debacle – it was one of the saddest, most maddening experiences of my life. We were faced with twelve professionals sitting round a large table in a room at the London Hospital. Each one in turn was called on to put their case, and justify to the room why they had – or had not – done certain things to help Jean Vialls. It transpired fairly quickly that Jean had been seen by four social workers. Each one of them had written a report detailing her circumstances and making various recommendations, but at no point had anybody actually taken any responsibility for her case or simply been her friend. Nobody had been prepared to arrange for someone to go each morning and give her a bath, for instance – until Jackie stepped up to the plate and took it on herself to care for her friend. The expert cancer consultant questioned the local GP.

'Why did you not tell me about this local problem? I passed Jean Viall's case on to you and you were responsible for her care.'

The GP looked up and replied, 'Your fax number had changed.'

We listened to the presentations for three quarters of an hour. At the end of the proceedings, I blew a fuse and banged my fist down hard on the table. It was a shocking moment for everyone in the room, myself included, but I simply could not contain my rage at what I'd heard. As far as I was concerned, given the tone and attitudes displayed that morning, the entire meeting was an exercise in face-saving on the part of the health-care professionals. Nobody gave any indication of honest remorse about Jean's death and nobody gave me any sense that the lessons arising from this terrible tragedy would be learned – Jean, even in death, was being treated as merely a point of business on an agenda, item number one, to be dealt with and moved swiftly on from. I told them as much. I also told them that if any one of them tried to run a business in this manner, with such lack of understanding or concern for their customers, they would go bankrupt within weeks.

For the next two hours we explored the nitty-gritty details: who had not spoken to whom; who had not taken responsibility for what; who had failed to pick up on what detail... I could only sit back and try to take in the exhaustive catalogue of failures.

This, then, was the NHS in action. Confusion, as rhetoric played out around the practical details of the final days of a young mother's life. It was heartbreaking to witness. In the past, as I had read newspapers and spoken to people of their experiences, I had tried to understand why it was that the NHS so often seemed to fail the people it is there to help. I, like many, had tried to do this by looking to Whitehall and the Department of Health, the macro level. But it was not until the tragedy of Jean Vialls that I began to understand at a micro level the problems of one of the largest organizations in the entire world.

All of the people in the room that day were, of course, incredibly well meaning. They did not wish any harm on Jean and were in the caring professions for extremely good reasons, probably to do with wanting to help and make a difference. Drowning in ideology and still chanting familiar mantras about health inequalities, somewhere along the way they had lost touch with the realities of the lives of the people with whom they were dealing – or were trying to work with structures that did not allow them to easily put into practice those things they knew would make a difference.

After a torturous meeting, four directors of different services came up to me, privately and individually, to tell me how much they agreed with what I was saying. None of them, though, could possibly express the same sympathy with me in public – their jobs, their livelihoods and those of their families were on the line, of course. Where was the person with courage enough to take a stand?

The core business of the welfare state was meant to be people like Jean and Jean's children. But somehow they had been forgotten about in the scramble to be able to demonstrate equality of opportunity, or efficiency of delivery, or equitable use of public monies. The NHS did not seem to understand who the customer was.

During the next three weeks, I worried deeply about what I'd heard and seen that day, and we started to formulate a plan for how we might be able to do things differently in Bromley-by-Bow – how we might take matters into our own hands and, in doing so, prevent another case of negligence on the scale of Jean Vialls. So, when I was called to attend a follow-up meeting in the wake of the inquiry into Jean's death, to discuss what could be done to ensure nothing like this could happen again in our area, I was ready. I was fast learning not to turn up at meetings with the public sector without a plan: otherwise I risked wasting hours on so much prevarication and hot air.

The plan, as I laid it out that day, was this: we would buy, for the princely sum of £1, the three acres of derelict land behind our buildings at the Centre, on which we would build the first integrated health centre in Britain. As with the nursery, this building would be built and owned by the people it was to serve, through a development trust. I took those assembled in the room on an imaginary journey through our health centre – entering through a cloister built around a landscaped garden, with a calming pond and a flowering Chinese tree. Walk further and you'd reach the threshold of the building itself, looking more like a barn than a traditional NHS primary care 'box'. Walk through the door and you would emerge into a light, open-plan reception area, which would double both as an art gallery, displaying and selling works of art, and as an events venue.

Our doctors would be able to offer their patients more than just drugs – they would be able to prescribe a hundred different activities each week, alongside the usual medical model of treatment. These would include art courses, access to community care, an allotment and countless other enterprising possibilities. Some patients would get the opportunity, through the health centre, to set up their own businesses. (I had noticed that Fifi, a West Indian mother, soon looked healthier when she was given support to set up her own hairdressing business. She got herself and her family off the Social Security they had previously relied on and began to get her life together. It seemed sensible to try and replicate this and to recognize that ill health and apathy were strongly connected.) Later, we would give patients access to education – through a Communiversity, plans for which were at that time in the offing. (We now have a student body of over seven hundred every year.) This whole process would connect health, education, housing, the environment, enterprise and the arts into one integrated project with one point of entry. Jean's problem had been the myriad agencies that had offered no 'joined-up' response to her needs. We would invent one.

We had imagined that our proposal for a new model of primary health care in an area without a decent basic facility would wow them – that the one body that would see the demand and be inspired by the way we proposed to supply the service would be the NHS. We were wrong. We might just as well have proposed a nuclear weapons facility for the area, given the respose we had from the health service. Instead of being excited, making useful suggestions or having a productive and creative exchange of ideas, we were stopped dead in our tracks. The response we received was one of ridicule – it was impossible to think of a state of affairs where one group of individuals took health-care provision into their own hands. It was inequitable! Once again, the preoccupation with equality for all only succeeded in maintaining the status quo. It had been fully ten years since our encounter in the original church building with the lady from Social Services with the encyclopaedia of reasons to stop innovation. It felt that the public sector had not moved an inch forward in ten years.

The NHS clearly had not come across social entrepreneurs before – and, as such, they were not prepared for the fact that we were not going to back down, lose confidence in our plan or disappear quietly from their field of vision. As I've said, social entrepreneurs tend to be tough, intransigent people. We love a fight and thrive in adversity. Eighteen months later, we were still no further forward. The NHS blocked our progress at every move. That was until one day I received a phone call from Dr Brian Mawhinney's office. Dr Mawhinney was the then Minister of State for Health in Margaret Thatcher's government. He'd heard about our problems, I was told, and he would like to come by and visit us. With nothing to lose, I suggested a date.

Early one brisk morning, three weeks later, I was opening the back door of the green ministerial car that had pulled up outside the church hall. Nobody emerged. I waited a few moments before poking my head inside. Nothing. Then someone gently tapped me on the back and pointed towards the figure of a man striding off with purpose down the street. 'The Minister,' I was told. Here was a man of action, I thought, and a fellow nosey parker to boot – off sniffing around already, sussing things out. I like him!

We eventually shook hands and I began the tour of the Centre. I told Jean's story and explained the frustrations I'd been experiencing in my dealings – my attempted dealings – with the NHS. He listened carefully and said little. Then he bid me farewell, got back in the car, and off he went. Righto, I thought. That's the last we'll hear of him.

Three weeks later, I received a letter bearing a Whitehall stamp. It contained a copy of a letter, signed by Dr Mawhinney, to the Chief Executive of the Health Authority, telling him (in no uncertain terms) to provide our health centre with a budget for three members of staff for three years, and to do it within the next thirty days. That straightforward, that uncompromising. It's a cliché to say it, but true: at that moment, it felt like a miracle. Yet again, it had taken just one person with sufficient clout, taking the time and being open-minded and long-sighted enough, to give us a chance and to be willing to take personal responsibility for the consequences. No excuses, no fudge and certainly no long-winded reports. Just a few lines in a letter, asking for a job to be done. And I had a hunch that he'd be making sure his requests were met. He would follow things through. It took a certain amount of courage for him to invest in us: after all, there was no guarantee that we'd succeed, there was no forerunner for what we were proposing. He'd only just met us.

I didn't meet Brian Mawhinney again for another ten years, but when I did I asked him what had happened after that visit all those years ago. He told me how a whole raft of civil servants had advised him against intervening in this local matter, that it was inequitable and unfair to do so, that it was poor practice and would undermine the health authority. Yet he had been appalled by the sense of inertia and prevarication that seemed to surround our situation. He had come into politics to make a difference, not to talk about making a difference, and he was consequently prepared to stick his neck out. I took pleasure in being able to report how his decision back then had paid off – that the rather dishevelled buildings he'd visited were now part of an internationally renowned suite of community buildings built over three acres, with a hundred staff and a hugely successful Healthy Living Centre which was redefining the approach to primary health care in the UK.

The social entrepreneur worth his or her salt will quickly learn how to take on the bastions of power, rise to a challenge, yet also protect themselves. The local NHS professionals were furious that we had succeeded in securing the Minister's backing. But, as I was discovering, government was a many-headed beast and we still had a struggle ahead of us if we were going to create a truly integrated development.

# taking it to scale

The health service agreed to give us a large grant towards the health centre, but we needed a significant additional sum before we had enough to get going. Just as if we were setting up a small business, we applied to the Norwich Union for a loan of £700,000, which we secured – the first non-GP practice in the UK to achieve such a loan at this time. We then secured a further grant, this time from the Department for the Environment, towards the redevelopment of the dishevelled parkland that backed on to our buildings.

We took out the loan; we lined up the health centre development, we were days away from starting work on the site and, just to make things less stressful, we were expecting the Prince of Wales at any day! He'd heard of our centre, and he wanted to see its inception for himself. The day before the Prince was due, my finance director Donald Findley came to give me some bad news: the Department of the Environment had pulled out. Without their backing we couldn't make the figures work. In short, we had a problem.

I wasn't what you'd call unfazed by this development, but I kept my nerve and, the next day, was showing Prince

Charles around the building site, introducing him to the residents of the area and my colleagues in our venture. His enthusiasm was obvious, he had a natural sympathy for what we were attempting to do. I think that he understood and responded to both our local focus and our entrepreneurial approach. Unlike many government ministers I have since met, he seemed, also, to be a man who was interested in and understood the practical details of the project. He appreciated the fact that we planned to use quality, sourced, natural materials in the fabric of our building, and that we would be encouraging local artists and craftspeople to participate. He even asked me where we had purchased the cobbles from for the park, a very practical question I have never been asked by any politician. He genuinely seemed to want to know, maybe because – probably unlike a lot of my other visitors – he had built a garden too. He knew to look for these details and understood that they were a source of pride to us (which illustrates my point: people who have learned about a thing by actually getting stuck in have a much richer understanding of the detail). I watched his enthusiasm grow and yet knew we could not now go ahead... It was galling. Eventually, I ventured to tell the prince about the difficulties we had just encountered. 'Leave it to me,' he said.

The next day I was presented with a copy of *The Times* newspaper and urged to read an article which made reference to a letter he had sent, in his 'spider' handwriting, to the then Secretary of State at the Department of the Environment, John Gummer, to express his concern for our predicament, his distress at hearing how their proposed funding had been withdrawn and suggesting that the

Secretary of State meet with us in person to discuss the matter further. Sure enough, within days I was called to a meeting at the minister's office.

Our meeting was very enlightening. Mr Gummer's concern, it seemed, was that our bid had been poorly written. I was taken aback by the comment – after all, we'd written it with the help of top officials from his very own department. 'We were guided by them in every aspect!' I told him, bluntly. 'And now you're telling me it was so badly done that it resulted in the funding being withdrawn? I have to admit, I'm a little confused...' The Permanent Secretary left the room to confirm that this was, in fact, the case. He returned a few minutes later, looking a little sheepish.

It was an embarrassing moment for us all, I think, but for Mr Gummer and his officials in particular. John was clearly sympathetic; he told me that if I resubmitted the document in the next round of funding, the following year, they would look at it again. 'And by the way,' he added by way of a post-script, 'don't mention the health centre this time: we're only dealing with the park.' Apparently, I later found out, our original bid had had a short and sorry life: it had ended up on the desk of a civil servant who had been very clear and punctilious about Sticking to the Rules. Scanning the paper, he had seen the words 'health centre' – that had been enough. Clearly this was nothing to do with him; this was one for the Department of Health. Out came the red pen and thus was our bid relegated to the 'no' pile.

And so, six months later, as requested, I re-submitted the exact same paper, with the exact same photographs and artists' drawings. I carefully deleted the two paragraphs that had mentioned the health centre. And, lo and behold, within a few weeks I had a call praising the fine application and offering the money.

This was in many ways a very difficult period for us but, as with every challenge, there were important lessons to be learned. As every social entrepreneur must, I was beginning to understand how to take on and tackle the governmental structures that stood in our way. I also learned that, as people like Bob Geldof have demonstrated, you have to be very clear about what you are trying to achieve; you have to be very bold in your approach, very vocal on behalf of your cause, and tirelessly persistent in your refusal to take no for an answer. When you do this, you begin to gather people to your cause, often from unexpected places.

There comes a point with any entrepreneur when, after painstakingly laying down roots and working on the detail on a very small-scale project, they begin to think about the larger canvas. An important characteristic of the social entrepreneur is the desire to get people to aspire to greater things. They want to raise expectations and offer people *more and better* than they can often even conceive of, because of their narrow range of experience or the kinds of role models available to them. When Jamie went into the kitchens at Kidbrooke and asked them what they wanted, the answer came: Chips! Pizza! In other words: more of the same. It was what they knew and there was no earthly reason to have expected them to want anything else. But he was determined to broaden their horizons and offer them more – in fact, he saw how critical it was that this happened, for the sake of their futures. Although this was not by any means easy (as anyone who saw the reactions of the children when confronted with a head of broccoli will recall), it was important and it challenged everyone involved – from the dinner ladies to the parents to the children themselves – to come up with creative ways of raising standards, challenging beliefs about themselves, changing attitudes, lifestyles and, eventually, changing lives.

This creativity and aspiration is at the heart of social entrepreneurship.

# getting into bed with business

earning to get into bed with business was no easy matter but was, it must be said, a somewhat less difficult endeavour than our experience with government had been so far. It was a learning curve that began for me in 1990 during a visit to Bromley by an organization called Business in the Community, which brings together a membership of companies who want to encourage businesses to improve their impact on social and environmental issues, to encourage achievement and success in the communities of which they are a part. A large coach trundled down the road towards us before disgorging thirty business people (mostly men) on to the street in front of the Bromley-by-Bow Centre. I showed them around and told them I needed help and support to develop the operation. To my surprise, they took me seriously and the visit resulted in me coming into contact with Libby Brayshaw, who eventually joined us on secondment from Royal Insurance for six months. Libby used her business skills to help us put together a plan to develop the three-acre park behind our buildings. She would end up staying with us for sixteen years, and even became a member of our board. It was incredibly exciting for me to make these initial bonds with business, and enormously rewarding to look back and see how strong and lasting they have proved to be.

Tesco joined us later, at a large multi-cultural meal that we held one evening in the church under the lovely candle-lit canopy. Ivor Lawrence was the manager at the time of the large Tesco store across the Blackwall Tunnel approach road. It was the nearest and biggest supermarket around. I had wanted to meet him for some time. He was an Essex lad, a bright man and a rising star in his business. Halfway through the evening – after enjoying the Bengali meal, the Burmese dancing, the West Indian poetry reading and the traditional English pudding – he turned to me with a question.

'Andrew. Do these people live around here?'

'Yes, of course they do, Ivor,' I replied. 'There are fifty different languages and dialects within a ten-minute walk of this building.'

'Hmm,' he said. And then added, eventually, 'Well, if this is who lives here... we're selling the wrong food.'

*Bingo!* I pointed out to Ivor that his supermarket had a fundamentally important part to play in the community. It was a place for social interaction and exchange. Many of the local Bengali women at this time were not integrating with other people, scared even to venture out of their flats. And this Asian community was growing – it now makes up 35 per cent of the total population of our area. I really felt that Tesco could, silly as it may have sounded at the time, play a crucial role in encouraging integration. Food, after all, unites people (as this evening was demonstrating). Ivor instantly made the connection between my social aims and his business interests and he agreed that Tesco would give us £27,000. We put the money towards renovating the derelict archway entrance to the new health centre, which had originally been designed by the eminent eighteenth-century architect William Kent (who famously designed Holkham Hall for the Earl of Leicester, and who landscaped Chiswick House and Horse Guards in Whitehall). In return, our Bengali staff would advise Tesco on social and food-related issues in the area, and we agreed to help him apply for planning permission for a new pharmacy that Tesco would run in their store.

At the time, and still often today, the attitude of much of the local voluntary sector and most of the churches was loud and clear – charity good, business bad. Yet here we were, supping with the devil and getting great social results.

# learning from Laura Ashley

**B**ack in Bromley-by-Bow, these were the kinds of things I was preoccupied with. One afternoon, I went off down the road to see my finance director, Donald. He had been looking at venues for me – I wanted to hold a staff conference. I wanted to take a group of local people and staff away somewhere fabulous – somewhere they wouldn't have envisaged themselves staying. I wanted them to aspire to greater things. I didn't want to take them to another public-sector-type environment – we all knew the score there. I wanted to give them an experience of grandeur, somewhere with history: somewhere they could get a sense of individuals from other times and places who'd had dreams and aspirations. As humans, we are profoundly influenced by environment and design – experiencing unexpected places lifts our expectations and aspirations and galvanizes our sense of what we're capable of.

I became particularly conscious of this when, in the early days at Bromley-by-Bow, David Ashley (the son of Laura Ashley) dropped by unexpectedly to see what we were up to. At the end of the visit, he had offered me the use of the Ashley house in Ryhader in Wales. Within two weeks I was leading a group of local people off on the road to Dyfed, without any sense of what we would find when we got there.

We drove slowly up a very narrow and winding lane approaching our destination and, eventually, we were rewarded with the sight of a magnificent large Welsh manor house in the distance. It stood alone, prominent halfway up a hill from which it surveyed the valley below. It was a glorious-looking place and as far removed from a council flat overlooking a flyover as you could have possibly imagined. For a lot of the people in the mini-van, the sense of awe went hand in hand with a sense of intimidation at its grandeur, the obvious fact that it was built with and for wealth and the wealthy.

We were greeted at the door by Emma Ashley who handed us the keys and left us to our own devices. As we walked through the rooms, I reminded the East Enders I was with that the Ashleys were an amazingly entrepreneurial family who had risen from humble beginnings in the 1950s – a £10 investment and one woman's desire to print her own fabric in her tiny flat had led to one of England's most successful and recognizable brands. Karen, a local mum who lived in a flat by the Blackwall Tunnel approach road, admitted that she was frightened to sleep in her bedroom when we first arrived. She was scared of so much silence – there were no ambulances racing up and down the dual carriageway outside. She found the quiet disturbing. Yet, after a few days away in this inspiring setting, with our own helipad on the back lawn, Karen's and all our mindsets had changed, and we were having entirely different conversations about ourselves, our homes and our plans for the future. This experience taught me just how profoundly true it is to say that we are products of the environments we live in. And it made me think that perhaps there was mileage to be had in thinking of a community project in terms of a successful family business.

Hence my visit to Donald to see how things were shaping up. Donald told me about the venue he'd had in mind – Allington Castle near Maidstone in Kent, which was currently owned by the Carmelite order. It was ideal, he said, but he'd just had bad news. It was up for sale; there was no way we'd be able to book it for our purposes. I looked at him a moment. This didn't strike me as bad news: it was an opportunity waiting to be seized. 'Why don't we buy it?' I said! Donald burst out laughing but he knew me better than to think it was a joke. That afternoon we climbed into my MG Roadster and set off for Kent.

Allington Castle is an eleventh-century medieval castle sitting on the banks of the river Medway in Kent. It was on the market for £2 million. Cost aside, it would be the perfect rural idyll and, conversation by conversation, our vision for its purpose took form. At our first meeting with Maidstone Council I was accompanied by Lord Ennals, a former Labour Minister and Patron of the Bromley-by-Bow Centre, and his wife Gene, who had worked with Dr Martin Luther King. The first thing they wanted to know was what exactly Maidstone had to do with the East End of London. It was a fair enough question and one I'd spent time thinking about. The economy of Maidstone, I was able to tell them, had historically been supported by the hard work of generations of East End labourers, who had traditionally, during the summer months, travelled to Kent to pick hops. We were simply looking to reconnect with this piece of shared history and rebuild common relationships between local people from urban and rural Britain. I had entertained a variety of different possible responses to my argument, but laughter had not been one of them – yet, to my astonishment, this was the immediate reaction. I was bemused, and a little embarrassed – what had I said? Thankfully it wasn't me they were laughing at. One of the councillors eventually gathered himself together enough to point at the wall behind me and ask, through the dregs of his chuckles, 'You haven't seen the picture?' I turned around and there above me, twenty feet by ten, was a large oil painting of East Enders picking hops. I literally couldn't have asked for a better illustration of my point. I believed I'd offered a convincing argument, with genuine social entrepreneurial concerns at its heart. It was good enough, at least, for them to let us go ahead and try to put together the money.

We tried our best but it was a lot to ask. After several months of hard slog, it was clear to us that we needed to persuade the owners to drop their price: it was the only way we could possibly afford to turn these buildings into a viable business proposition. The property was going to soak up thousands of pounds in necessary renovations alone. We put our case yet again, arguing that the buildings had been used for charitable and religious purposes for several hundred years and that they should not simply be sold off to the highest private bidder. Much better that they go to another charitable body that would fulfil its historic purpose.

We had the vision and the energy but, sadly, we were not able to win the day this time. An American businessman with a gigantic bank balance became interested and bought the castle outright, after all our efforts at the coalface. We were out of the picture.

I wanted to relate this story because it demonstrates a good point about social entrepreneurship. We didn't achieve our goal at Allington, but the process had taught us a lot. We had raised our aspirations and confidence as a direct result of all the hard work and research we'd invested; our entrepreneurial skills had been tested and honed. We had learned how to turn problems into potential opportunity by not allowing ourselves to reduce our horizons. And, indeed, one day we would realize the vision we'd had for the castle, when in 1996 the opportunity came to take over the running of a fifteen-bedroom manor house in the Cotswolds. Stanton Guildhouse had been built in the sixties by one Mary Osborn – who had lived just down the road from us in Bromley-by-Bow, ironically at Kingsley Hall! Mary's vision for this house had been a charitable one – that it should be built by, and for, the local population. The interior of the house still features many examples of fine local craftsmanship. In her lifetime the house was visited by a number of famous names, including John Betjeman and J. B. Priestley. Today, we have on display a personal letter that Mahatma Gandhi wrote to Mary, as well as a spinning wheel which had been presented to Gandhi on his sixty-fifth birthday. Stanton Guildhouse is now run as a social enterprise on clear business principles with a clear social purpose. It is enjoyed not only by business people and the public sector, but also by the voluntary and charitable sectors, and members of the general public; not only by local people but also by international bodies; not only by the wealthy but also by the less well off. It has a sustainable business plan.

# the arrival of New Labour

B y 1997, back in east London, the health centre was nearing completion and the general election campaign that would famously bring New Labour into power was well under way. We had all come a long way and the feeling of optimism in Britain was palpable. 'Community' was at the heart of the New Labour project. Indeed, their election manifesto solemnly and defiantly stated that they wanted to earn the faith of 'the broad majority of people who work hard, play by the rules, pay their dues and feel let down by a political system that gives the breaks to the few, to an elite at the top increasingly out of touch with the rest of us'. They were directly identifying themselves as 'one of us' – not 'one of them'. It seemed there was reason to be hopeful. As for the NHS, they saw the need for change: 'there must be flexibility, not rigid prescription, if innovation is to flourish', they told us.

The bonds of community were seen a source of social good in and of themselves, but also as a tool for regeneration and renewal. Tony Blair made this the theme of his very first speech as Prime Minister in June 1997, delivered at Aylesbury Estate in Southwark. Spelling out the new government's commitment to tackling social exclusion, he announced the possibility of a new 'alliance between the haves and the have-nots', between those with the means to exclude themselves voluntarily, by buying out, and those who were automatically excluded by poverty or lack of opportunity. The PM's speech set out a clear vision by promising that New Labour would 'back thousands of "social entrepreneurs"... who bring to social problems the same enterprise and imagination that business entrepreneurs bring to wealth creating... people on every housing estate who have it in themselves to be community leaders'. His government would 'find out what works... support the successes and stop the failures... back anyone – from a multinational company to a community association – if they can deliver the goods'.

In Bromley-by-Bow we had not forgotten the last months of Jean's life: they were a horror story of incompetence and raised profound questions about the way in which health care was in danger of losing its humanity. Our vision for the new health centre was committed to a truly integrated care system whose team approach would involve not only health professionals, social workers, education experts, project staff and volunteers but also artists and musicians; that funding would go to high-quality, innovative, entrepreneurial projects that genuinely responded to the needs of the community, so that people might take active ownership of their health rather than simply being passive patients and victims. New Labour, too, was keen to right some wrongs and, sure enough, one day I was contacted by Peter Mandelson's office.

The caller told me that New Labour was going to launch a new policy as part of its election campaign – a green paper on public health, *Our Healthier Nation*, in which they were going to propose a network of healthy living centres aimed at improving health among the poorer communities. According to the then Minister for Public Health, Tessa Jowell, these community projects, partly funded by a new National Lottery fund called the New Opportunities Fund (NOF), would 'belong to the communities that they serve and not be parachuted in from Whitehall' and, since they would be considering Bromley-by-Bow as a prototype, I was being called on to outline the key concepts behind the venture.

The concept of the healthy living centre at Bromley-by-Bow, I told them, was to set health in an integrated social context, where a holistic attitude to clinical services would mean that a whole range of services or activities could be offered to the community of users. The Centre was founded on the pillars of health and social care, education and train-ing, employment and enterprise, the environment and the arts. Our aim was to empower local people to make choices and ultimately take responsibility for their own lives. It was run by a committed integrated team of people working col-lectively, rather than simply co-locating their services on the same site. New Labour, it seemed, agreed wholeheart-edly with the approach – indeed the green paper, when it was published, included a foreword, written by Tony Blair himself, in which he stated:

I believe that by working together, we can tackle poor
health, and achieve the aim of better health for everyone,
and especially for the least fortunate... Individuals taking
action for themselves and their families are central to this.

Communities working together can offer real help. And there is a vital role for Government too. Not as the so-called nanny state in action, but the Government addressing the big issues which affect our health, like housing, jobs and education.

Bromley-by-Bow's was the first fully integrated health centre in the UK, bringing together GPs, nurses, arts, education, a three-acre park, sheltered housing, support and care in one fully unified unit at the hub of the community. Life itself is an integrated experience – it stands to reason that in order to assess the health of a person in Bromley-by-Bow or any other inner-city area, it would be necessary to deal with every aspect of that person's life, to take a holistic view of the individual in his or her particular environment, living in his or her particular *community*.

We even began to implement various schemes, through our Healthy Living Centre, designed to demonstrate both its scope and our ambition for its future. We set up a food co-op, for example – a resource that our GPs could draw on and 'prescribe' to their patients. Jointly funded by the health and local authorities – and way before Jamie came on the scene – the co-op enabled local people to buy fresh fruit and vegetables much more cheaply than in the shops. We also established a welfare and benefits advice shop, so that visitors to the health centre could seek help with problems relating to housing, social security, benefits and any other welfare matter causing them to suffer emotionally and materially. (Because we had spent many years in the area, living among the community, we knew that ill health often had its roots in social problems, or other dilemmas that could not be helped with a spoonful of syrup taken three times a day with food.) We offered yoga, t'ai chi, aromatherapy, dance classes for children, exercise classes for Bengali women, individually tailored exercise programmes for older people with arthritis or heart or respiratory problems, circuit training for the local boys (a great way, it turned out, to focus energy and pent-up anger in positive ways).

# building a sense of 'place'

**E**ver since I had been in Bromley-by-Bow, and met and worked with people like Su and Margy, I had become a passionate believer that there should be a very important role for the arts in developing and maintaining the health of the inner city. Art and artists are inspiring – they literally (I've seen it happen!) make dreams come true, they offer ways of expressing complicated feelings, they are nurturing of creativity. They can open up whole new horizons for people who might feel they have very few. They make a place look nice. They make people feel good about themselves.

Art projects can break the patterns of failure with which places like Bromley-by-Bow become associated, by raising expectations and encouraging people to look at their situation with fresh eyes. When that happens, something really exciting begins to emerge: local people become confident partners in the process of change. When the Centre was up and running, we wasted no time in offering people art classes and art projects to join in with. With art as the medium, everyone was given the opportunity to realize unfulfilled potential through contact with other people and cultures: art can offer a way in which to transcend race, age, disability, gender, education and quite a lot of cultural hostility. Today, walking through the Centre, you're likely to see local residents helping to run art classes for physically and mentally disabled members of their community; or workshops being run through the Centre to demystify and communicate information about health through art; recently, we ran a singing course for young asthma sufferers, to help with breathing techniques.

We have always focused on working with practising artists rather than art teachers. Our artists make high demands on the people they work with; they don't tolerate mediocrity or half-heartedness. One of our longest-serving members of staff at the centre is Sheenagh McKinlay, our stained-glass artist and tutor in our Community Care projects. For many years Sheenagh has worked with clients with profound disabilities and as she strives for perfection in her own art, so too does everyone she works with. People like Sheenagh are the social entrepreneurs of the art world, pushing themselves and those they work with to be the best they can be. In Bromley-by-Bow we have a rich heritage of such artists: from Santiago Bell to Frank Creber, from Sheenagh McKinlay to our renowned stone carver Paula Haughney.

Many of their works of art have been used in the buildings and gardens. They instil a sense of beauty and inspiration, in stark contrast to the cheap, largely degenerate environment of the surrounding area that only reinforces the endemic sense of failure (and in remarkable contrast to the buildings as they were when I first arrived!). The physical and emotional environment of the Centre has been designed to reflect the high value placed on the people who use it and is based on integration, creativity and excellence.

A good example of our approach to community involvement arose when we came to redevelop the park and
brought in one of the best garden designers in the country
to work with the residents of Bromley-by-Bow to transform
the derelict space – what ensued was a transfer of energy,
ideas and inspiration. Around that time I had a visit from
Billy, a twenty-eight-year-old unemployed builder. He could-
n't get a job on a building site any more, he told me, because
he suffers from rare bouts of epilepsy; he'd only had one fit
in the last six years. But, as a result, nobody would touch
him, they didn't want to take the risk, and he and his family
were, quite literally by the looks of him, wasting away.
Things were very difficult for Billy and he was seen by Social
Services as a 'person with problems', costing the state thousands of pounds a year in medication for depression alone.
As we were talking, he expressed a keen interest in what was
going on in the park, and went off on a very passionate flight
of fancy about how it would be great to plant a meadow
there. Hmm, I thought, listening to his vision – that would
indeed be great. To his surprise, I told him I thought it was a
superb idea, and that he should go for it. I'd give him a pick
and shovel, and whatever funds he required to get the material he needed to get started. Once he realized I was
serious – and was taking him very seriously indeed – he
wasted no time in getting to work. Within weeks, a whole
area once covered in tarmac had been dug over and Billy
had begun to sow wild flowers and grasses. It was great to
watch!

Over time, as the meadow grew, it became a real joy of a
place to sit in. It attracted all kinds of people – the elderly
population in particular was drawn there to sit and chat and

watch the butterflies which the meadow had also attracted to this rundown part of town. Billy's dream had promoted a whole new colourful and optimistic community feeling – it made people feel like they were worth something, worth better.

And for Billy himself, rebuilding the park helped him rebuild his life and his family's lives. He was soon running the park full time, which today works fantastically well – Billy's a big guy, well respected, certainly not someone you want to get on the wrong side of, and the kids who might have thought about vandalizing that kind of a community space think twice when they realize who they'll have to answer to. Giving Billy just that little sense of autonomy and personal responsibility made the most amazing difference, both to him personally and to our whole community. The success of this venture has been phenomenal – we saw in it the potential to set up a gardening business, which we did. Green Dreams, as we called it, is a social enterprise that is transforming public spaces across east London and is turning over half a million pounds in business every year.

# the dinosaur exposed

When New Labour came to power, as promised it established the £300 million lottery fund to back its policy of establishing healthy living centres up and down the country. I was pretty excited and thought it might be helpful if I was to meet with the fund's Chief Executive, and bring along one of our progressive GPs, Sam Everington (who would eventually become the Vice-Chairman of the British Medical Association) to share the benefit of our knowledge and practical experience – such as it was, it was surely worth something to him.

We joined him for a meal arranged by Geoffrey Tucker, one of the best business networkers in the country and a truly great supporter of our work. It seemed sensible that if funding was to be put towards replicating the kind of healthy living centre we'd established in Bromley-by-Bow then the general entrepreneurial principles which lay behind its successful operation might be helpful to other similar ventures. I was absolutely clear that making these centres sustainable was a big question, an important one, and that I had some ideas of how this might be done successfully. I also knew that Tony Blair was very keen on finding what, at the time, he was calling a 'Third Way' –

which he defined, in a Fabian Society pamphlet published in 1998, as the 'reappraisal of social democracy, reaching deep into the values of the Left to develop radically new approaches'. I was not partisan in the least bit, but I would go and talk with anyone who seemed interested in making a positive movement towards repositioning the state's role as one of guarantor, rather than provider, of public services.

The CEO's background was in the civil service and during the meeting we were rather disappointed to be told that the social entrepreneurial approach we were proposing as the best possible model for the successful implementation of healthy living centres across the UK would be considered as only one approach – that, of course, the fund was concerned to be 'fair' in its approach and would seek to encompass a wide range of different ideas and schemes that it would *then* brand as healthy living centres. We want to treat people fairly, he said. Geoffrey's response summed it up for us all: 'Oh... *Really...*' he said, with a wry smile.

It was at this very point that, for me, alarm bells began to ring. Experience had taught me that without a coherent sustainable plan, things quickly begin to unravel. It was ironic, I thought, that money raised from gambling should be pumped into businesses built on individuals taking a punt. My argument at the time is my argument today: why not put that money behind people who had already taken the risk – fairly successfully, as it turned out – and who had business experience, who could apply their knowledge to the setting up of enterprises in social sector? At the time this was the only charitable fund which had a rationale that could justify it being used in this way. Quite simply put: we were a good investment! It was not to be. We took the money that they were offering towards the Bromley-by-Bow Centre, backed away, and waited to see what would happen next.

A national representative committee was duly created, comprising twelve people, none of whom had any previous experience setting up an integrated healthy living centre. They set in motion a bureaucratic public-sector process designed to share out the lottery money equally between 257 healthy living centres across the UK – centres whose ethos and ways of working had about as much in common with each other as chalk and cheese. As the saying goes, all of them would get a lick but none of them would have a meal. Five years on, in 2002 – a full turn of the funding cycle – virtually all of the money had been spent and I was approached by a large consultancy firm. Their representative told me that that they were bidding to the National Lottery Fund to put together a rescue package for the 257 healthy living centres – many of them had proved not to be sustainable, they were running out of money and several million pounds of further lottery funds were going to be invested in an attempt to rescue some of them. They had heard, I was told, that we in Bromley-by-Bow were the people to talk to about all of this stuff, that we had the kind of experience they clearly needed to draw on. I had to laugh. Another circle, then, had been turned.

I joined the consultancy's team and we won the bid. For a short time I worked with business colleagues to put together a rescue package. Part of the attempt was to focus on enabling them to thrive as stand-alone social enterprises but actually it seemed too late – a great deal of money had been spent on schemes that were simply not sustainable. In an article entitled 'Series of wasteful initiatives end up doing fat lot of good' in *The Times* in February 2006, Nigel Hawkes, Health Editor, reported:

[The Government's plans] to tackle obesity, including the Healthy Schools programme, the Safe and Sound Challenge, Healthy Living Centres and exercise on prescription... had little effect and have now, mostly, been forgotten. Healthy Living Centres absorbed £300 million of lottery money before subsiding unhealthily into oblivion. Exercise on pre-scription never appealed to GPs and has been little used. Since 1999 obesity has continued to rise, prompting the promise made in 2004 that the upward curve would be halted by 2010.

I have recently been asked to develop further some of my original thinking about how to develop healthy living centres successfully, but it makes me sad that an opportu-nity to develop a seriously entrepreneurial venture, which would have fitted in perfectly with what was being asked now, had been missed, as well as the money wasted. Confused ideas about fairness, legislation which repeated old approaches, lack of leadership, shortage of evidence and sheer drift had ended up delivering nothing but a mess, and if an idea doesn't deliver instant results, politicians consign it to the big out-tray in the sky. This happens time and time again. The result is that nobody has really taken ownership of the idea, or has the time to pursue it with the kind of determination it requires. No one had bothered to stay around long enough to watch, or learn really important lessons – lessons which actually have implications for bil-lions of pounds of public-sector spending.

At a recent conference in Birmingham, a senior lottery official told us that he had been trying for two years now to talk to the Secretary of State for Health about the healthy living centre venture but had consistently failed to find anyone willing to meet and discuss it. He, no less than us, was caught up in the tangled net of government processes.

During the course of this saga ministers and civil servants alike kept telling me that they were accountable for public money. Darren, a young East End entrepreneur on our estate, was interested in learning more about the healthy living centres and, one day, I took him along to join us at a meeting with a senior minister. He listened to the talk and when I asked him what he thought afterwards, he said, 'I wouldn't even give that bloke a fiver – he'd lose it!' He wasn't wrong.

The healthy living centre experience was the first of what is now a number of attempts we have made to move from the micro to the macro along business lines, to grow new responses to the failure of public-sector delivery. I realized it was only a matter of time before the same civil servants who had picked up on our ideas, dumbed them down, missed all the opportunities and wasted a great deal of money along the way, would begin to blame us – the entrepreneurs – and our ideas, which clearly, from their point of view, did not work in practice. The reality, however, was that these public-sector officials were precisely the wrong people to try to implement our ideas in the wider sphere – many of them came from academic backgrounds and operated within a strict set of processes that could never allow these social enterprises to grow as *real* enterprises.

The next attempt to take the experience of the Bromley-by-Bow Centre and put it on to a national platform was the National Health Service's Local Improvement Finance Trust (LIFT). This public-private finance initiative is investing in excess of £2 billion in the building and development of new integrated primary health and social care facilities across England and, yet again, our Centre was held up as an example of all that it could achieve in practice.

I worked closely with the civil servants who developed much of the rationale behind the scheme. I spoke at meetings up and down the land, cajoling and encouraging GPs to embrace this new opportunity. I had huge misgivings about this new venture, but I was prepared to engage with it nonetheless – we needed to be pragmatic. Along with the Community Action Network, we worked with GSL Global Solutions to promote our model of delivery and secure the first £30 million LIFT contract in east London, a contract which gave them control over the development of key primary care facilities in the area for the next twenty-five years. In turn, this would allow our team to influence the process. The former CEO of the Bromley-by-Bow Centre, Paul Brickell, eventually became the chairman of the east London LIFT company (and now chairs two LIFT companies, responsible for building fifteen health centres). We want to be involved, because the scheme is so full of possibility and has the potential to propagate our ideas and experience.

Today LIFT is well under way but many of the schemes have a long way to go. Co-location of services is beginning to happen in some of the separately managed health centres, but few have yet got as far as we have, embracing a fully integrated approach managed by one team of people.

# inside out

**A**llison Trimble joined me as a community worker in the early nineties. She had worked with the charity Christian Aid with people suffering from leprosy in India. Now back in Britain, she wanted to work with real people, not behind a desk in the office of a charity, and when she arrived on her first day, I greeted her with a smile on my face and a ladder in my hand and asked her if she'd help put up some bunting on Bruce Road for a street fair we were holding – one of the first of many. Allison had a real feel for people and great empathic insight into the lives and problems of local residents. She understood the inner dynamics of the dependency culture that dominated the lives of many people in the surrounding estates. Allison had a cunning idea. We were in need of help; there were a lot of very capable, strong, bright people on our doorstep who could make a big difference but were caught in the benefit trap and not allowed to earn other monies. She was clear that we needed to use an economic incentive to entice local people to work in community care – thereby taking more responsibility for themselves and their surrounding communities. The £5 we decided to offer towards expenses to volunteers at the project came just within the rules.

Our Community Care project very gradually took root. It began to create a rhythm to the day for many people – a small financial incentive but, more importantly, a reason for people to come together and care for each other. It was my view at the time that the scale of the problems in this kind of an area were beyond the capabilities of any single individual – myself, a social worker, a well-meaning vicar... Not one of us on our own could save the day and, in fact, most people charged with the task were immediately overwhelmed, closed their office doors and hid from view. We needed to develop a communal response and, by learning to take care of each other, lessen the dependence on professionals.

The Community Care project has been running for sixteen years now and I have seen it become the route through which countless local people have gone on to get themselves out of the benefits quagmire, finding work both within the Centre and beyond. Today, over 60 per cent of the Centre's staff is drawn from the local community and hundreds of others have found a route into employment through the opportunities that we have provided.

When the author Germaine Greer heard of us, she asked if she could come and spend three days working with and listening to the people in our community. She wanted to participate in Community Care sessions, mix with our artists and generally get a feel for what was actually happening. After the three days were up, I was keen to hear what conclusions she'd come to.

'Andrew, what's happening here is not a "top-down" approach, and neither is it a "bottom-up" approach. What's happening here is "inside-out".'

I wasn't sure I followed, and asked her to explain.

She told me about having met Zenith Rahman, a Bengali mother who had come to me early on with an idea for setting up a project to help local families build connections and support networks. As with Billy, I'd thought it was a brilliant idea and encouraged the passion she clearly had for the venture, giving her the money to get started. (Zenith is a wonderful woman, completely hands-on and no-nonsense – a very smart business-like woman, in fact.) Germaine told me how, by nurturing this talent and protecting it from all the forces which, in an area like this, might have stood in its way, we had enabled Zenith to create a successful project in an environment where very often things fail. As a direct result, Zenith formed relationships with a whole new set of people, out of which other ventures emerged, and those in turn have ignited countless projects transforming the lives of hundreds of the most vulnerable in our community. This approach, Germaine explained, can be seen as an 'inside-out' approach because it starts with one person and their particular passion.

She was completely right – I'd never thought we had such a clear 'approach' because so much of what we'd built had developed over the years mainly through instinct, trial and some error. Germaine had painted for me an organic picture of our work, and offered an insight which genuinely felt affirming and energizing.

In an article entitled 'Art that Heals the Inner Being' for the *Financial Times* following her visit, Germaine contrasted the famous (notorious, even) Royal Academy's 'Sensations' exhibition, which featured work from the Saatchi collection (including artists such as Damien Hirst and Tracy Emin), with the artistic approach she'd seen in practice during her time at the Bromley-by-Bow Centre. She described the pieces at the Royal Academy's exhibition as 'short sharp blasts of heightened awareness. It is art of a consumerist culture that finds nothing worth waiting for and no pleasure in anticipation'. She then described a self-portrait of a young local Turkish mother of two, Togrol, which hung in the Health Centre at Bromley. It depicted a woman 'with dark-lashed blue eyes and dark hair hanging in thick wedges'. Germaine had found the image very arresting and had asked more about its subject.

Togrol was paralysed from the chest down in a hit-and-run accident, abandoned by her husband and deprived of her children. When the volunteer first brought her out of the disabled flat she hadn't left for months, and introduced her to the mosaic group, she sat silent in her wheelchair, unmoved and unmoving.

Through the careful support and friendship of local volunteers, she began to participate in the classes and, piece by piece, she created this self-portrait.

As the picture took shape, Togrol began to speak. By the time it was finished, she was talking and joking as freely as the others. Now she lives independently, has a job and has moved out of the borough. Togrol's great adventure was her struggle back to life.

Art, not for consumption but as it was always meant to be: for, and about, *life*.

Germaine concluded her article with these words:

Bromley Centre is being recognised in some circles as a pathfinder scheme that could provide the model of inner-city regeneration... If the success [...] is to be replicated elsewhere, the professionals will have to find in themselves the same combination of patience and humility that characterises the workers at Bromley-by-Bow. Humility is no more than the realisation that every single other person, no matter how deprived, confused or crushed, is at least as valuable and important as oneself.

# insight from down under

I expected an Oxbridge Anglican priest with an Australian accent – someone, I imagined, very reserved. The person who slapped me on the back with a hearty 'How are you?' was a down-to-earth Aussie who called a spade a dirty great shovel. I liked him immediately and he was like no other Anglican priest I'd ever met! When Tony Blair became Prime Minister I was invited to hear Peter speak – he was, apparently, Blair's 'guru'. Peter was nervous. He was very close to Tony and he didn't want to upset the apple cart – and he was a 'foreigner' to boot. He didn't want the limelight. He presented his paper on the future of the church and he talked a lot about the influence of the theologian John McMurray on his life and thinking. McMurray understood the importance of community, friendship and mutual relationships as being core to human development and freedom. I listened to the discussion that ensued. I found I warmed to everything Peter had to say. I told the gathered group that what Peter had just described was a very accurate description of the philosophy of the Bromley-by-Bow Centre which we had been developing for some years. We'd never heard of McMurray, but Peter Thomson seemed to be on to something.

For me, he was another Santiago figure – older and wiser than me, but someone in whom I felt I could trust and confide. Peter often told me how far removed Tony Blair's world was from the kinds of practical reality I was familiar with at Bromley-by-Bow, and that Peter felt a responsibility to remind him of some of these realities. And I, in turn, felt a responsibility to expose Peter to as many of the realities of the work of social entrepreneurs around Britain as I possibly could. I wanted to help him see and understand what the public and voluntary sectors were up to. Peter understood very quickly. 'Shit, mate, what are these liberals on about?'

The more he saw of the detail, the more he became convinced that this practical environment in Bromley-by-Bow and other places provided a very different insight into 'macro' policy and into the Prime Minister's desire for change. He saw that by championing 'fairness', Tony Blair would get nowhere in his quest for social change. In fact, the reverse could occur. Motives and consequences are very different things and New Labour appeared to believe that if the public sector embraced the right values then somehow the right practical consequences would follow. But without understanding the detail of practice at the coalface of the community, the goods would simply not be delivered.

ACCEPTING THE CHALLENGE

# building the road as you walk it

The journey which resulted in the creation of the Bromley-by-Bow Centre has been long and challenging, sometimes even arduous, but I don't believe I have ever undertaken a more rewarding and important journey in my entire life. I am fond of using the phrase 'building the road as you walk it' and this is because so much of my experience has been about doing just this. What I find so thrilling today is just how far we have come, and how much we have learned.

Despite all the setbacks, our work is becoming better known and its impact more widely recognized. As I have outlined, we have frequently been used by government as an example of what they have believed many of their policy announcements could mean in practice. The following examples, some of which I've mentioned in the story so far, will give you a flavour:

*Our Healthier Nation: a contract for health*
**Government Green Paper, February 1998**
This Green Paper stated the Government's intention to support the development of healthy living centres. The Green Paper (section 3.66) contains a description of the

Bromley-by-Bow Centre as an example of the concept in action. The subsequent White Paper (*Saving Lives: Our Healthier Nation*, July 1999) announced that the New Opportunities Fund would fund a nationwide programme of healthy living centres.

## Social exclusion

Alistair Darling MP, Secretary of State for Social Security, launched the Government report *Opportunity for all — tackling poverty and social exclusion* at the Bromley-by-Bow Centre on 21 September 1999.

## Neighbourhood renewal

The Social Exclusion Unit Policy Action Team 18 (PAT 16) report *Learning Lessons* was launched at the Bromley-by-Bow Centre in March 2000 by Lord Falconer, Cabinet Office Minister.

## Sustainable regeneration

The development of the Bromley-by-Bow Centre's parkland was cited as an example of good practice in *Sustainable Regeneration: a good practice note* (Department of Environment, Transport and the Regions).

## Social enterprise

'There are now a range of organisations moving to become social enterprises. We all know the work of the Bromley-by-Bow Centre in London's Docklands based on the philosophy of communities working together.' Patricia Hewitt, Secretary of State for Trade and Industry, 6 February 2002, NCVO Annual Conference.

## Children's Centres

The Bromley-by-Bow Centre was in the first tranche of thirty-two Children's Centres in the country. The Children's Centre programme was launched at the Bromley-by-Bow Centre on 23 June 2003 by Margaret Hodge MP, Minister for Children, and Charles Clarke MP, Secretary of State for Education, who cited the Centre as one of 'the best examples of joined up early years services'.

## Health Inequalities

*Health Inequalities — A Programme for Action* was launched at the Bromley-by-Bow Centre by John Reid MP, Secretary of State for Health, on 2 July 2003. He said, 'The Bromley-by-Bow Centre... is an innovative model of integrated services which helps to overcome many of the traditional obstacles to good healthcare in deprived inner-city areas'.

## NHS LIFT

The LIFT programme has already been mentioned above. It is worth noting that Dr Sam Everington, one of the Bromley-by-Bow Centre's Principal GPs, was chosen as a National Director of Partnerships for Health, and the Centre is the primary model for this £2 billion programme. Professor Paul Brickell, one of the former Chief Executives of the Centre, is the Chair of the east London LIFT company, which was the first in the country. These developments will have a profound effect on primary care throughout the country and could play a major role in regenerating local communities.

## Primary care

In the 2006 Health White Paper, the Bromley-by-Bow Centre

was cited as having a cutting-edge approach to providing community services: 'an excellent example of a centre providing a range of services, all co-located. People can see a GP then have a healthy meal, get information about other services and sign up for a course or exercise programme all in one place'.

## Awards

I was awarded an OBE in the Millennium New Year Honours List for my work in Bromley-by-Bow, and in 2002 I was invited by Tony Blair to join the Prime Minister's Delivery Unit to advise on public-service delivery. In 2007 I was awarded a life peerage and now sit on the cross benches in the House of Lords.

Our challenge now – and the challenge I pose throughout this book – is this: will people let us be more than just a great example? Will they trust our expertise, our experience, gained over so long working both at grass-roots level and with policy advisers, and give us the means to make real change happen? Or will they put their money and faith in the hands of people without experience, and ask them to move mountains to produce instant results?

# giving the emperors
# back their clothes

Think back to Tony Blair's words, delivered in Southwark, about backing social entrepreneurs. His vision was highly ambitious: it sought to systemize and make national the most dynamic, fluid and intangible qualities of successful community organizations, and to link them to the most general objectives of a government for society – dignity, activity, wealth and progress. On top of that, it challenged some highly cherished principles about equity, risk management and democratic accountability that are strongly defended by many politicians and public-sector officials – often in the face of evidence that they simply do not deliver for the poorest communities in the country. In particular, social enterprise suggests that power and decision-making in disadvantaged neighbourhoods might be more productively vested in individuals or groups who 'can deliver', rather than in representative, elected committees and boards. Starting with people rather than theory, or structure, social enterprise challenges the prevailing notion of what constitutes democratic legitimacy. Social enterprise is, therefore, rather more honest than might be comfortable to many in Whitehall about the failure of the existing representative structures of local government to involve, or even interest, the great majority of the population.

The vision was a great one. But early on it was clear to me that the dream was not being followed through. His rhetoric suggested a radical entrepreneurial approach, but the practice in programmes such as Sure Start and, as I've shown, healthy living centres, focused more on management than enterprise, more on formal representation than on direct practical involvement and, yet again, more on short- than on long-term vision. New Labour seemed set on creating what colleagues of mine have called 'communities in committee', which have so often been stifled by the institutional forms on which they rely. Instead, I believe we need 'communities in business', which would remain true to Tony Blair's original vision: but few in New Labour, then or now, understand the detail of this, or have even demonstrated an interest in wanting to understand.

The real tragedy is that, broadly speaking, the areas of deprivation in the UK have not shifted a great deal since Dickens's day, and any talk of a new approach of the kind I fervently believe would work has led us to nothing but lots of strategizing, meetings, papers, conferences, seminars, websites... and when the money runs out, there is nothing left to show, no tangible result and so, of course, the show moves on.

I am reminded of the 364 economists who wrote a letter to *The Times* in the early eighties advising Margaret Thatcher and Geoffrey Howe not to go down the path of monetarism. All their research was telling them that the economy would collapse and inflation rise through the roof. The Vice-Presidents of the Royal Economic Society all put their name to that letter, as did seventy-six different professors and promising young dons. The country was in a hole, they warned, and Howe's policies would only dig it deeper...

They had all taught – or been taught – that government had to spend money to keep the economy going. That was the Chancellor's job. Howe, though, bucked the trend by positively slashing his spending plans. Within weeks of his 1981 budget, the economy began to look rather perky. This budget has come to be seen as the crucial turning point in a previously sorry story of the British economy. During an interview on *Newsnight* Lord Howe described these 364 'experts' as people who could tell you 364 ways to make love, without any one of them having actually had sex.

Across the country, people are growing weary of traditional methods of community consultation and community governance, which have failed to engage their interest or commitment, or make any real changes to their lives. Places like Bromley-by-Bow have grown up out of this frustration, engaging large sections of local communities in their own regeneration – but our approach cannot be drawn up as a Cabinet Office blueprint and then standardized across the country. They need to be given the freedom to develop in the way that works best in their particular setting. Nevertheless, lessons can very definitely be learned from them, and guidelines and principles of best practice drawn up. If these principles are supported consistently, then we could probably make a national programme of 'neighbourhood renewal' into a realistic ambition.

Tony Blair started out on the right track, in his speech, by grasping the message of the social entrepreneur. For his part, David Cameron has described the importance of overlaps between the government's promotion of social enterprise and the social responsibility agenda of the Conservative Party as 'the Big Idea for Britain's Future'. As he struggles to flesh out the bones of his new thinking – attempting to get hold of the 'grit', as he rightly calls it – one can sense David Cameron struggling to understand a world of which he has little personal, long-term experience. My advice to David would be to focus on a few examples of mature social enterprise that have got hold of the details, worked with the material for many years, and not to be driven by a marketing agenda which can so easily, like a butterfly, flit from leaf to leaf in search of the sun.

Civil servants have been discouraged from focusing on any one place, or any one job, for too long. Conversely, I would actively encourage this approach, for it is in understanding one place in great detail (focusing on the micro) that the demands of the macro will be understood. Gordon Brown or David Cameron or anyone else wishing to take over the mantle at the next election and seriously engage with regeneration would do well to consult with one or two well-established social enterprises before they speak too confidently about what should be done on a national scale. The way into the macro is the micro, as any business person worth their salt will tell you.

If I were the minister responsible for enterprise, I would identify fifteen people who have shown that they can deliver results in practice. I would imagine they would all be pretty challenging people – the John Birds, Bob Geldofs and Alan Sugars of this world. I would invite them to sit down with me in a room and tell them that I was giving each of them £3 million to invest in working in a particular poor, deprived area. One year later, I would invite them back into the room. Those who had messed up would get no more money; those who showed promise would get another £3 million; and those who had done really well would get £10 million. In other words, I would back success and build on what actually works. I would endeavour for the most part to keep civil servants and academics at a distance and I would certainly ensure that no more than 5 per cent of what monies we had available went towards evaluation. However, I would not for one moment underestimate the importance of evaluation. To that end, I would choose another group of successful entrepreneurs and business people to carry out research on how projects were performing by using all of the available technology and by trusting them to use the best methodology for their purpose. I would want to see very practical results being delivered and I would want local people to be involved in the process. Entrepreneurs smell success: they do not write reports about it.

My approach might well be thought of as being over-simplified and even crass. Given the uncertainties and ideological cleavages over the future shape of the public-service market, and over the likely balance of provision across public, private and third sectors, it is not surprising that the prospect of social enterprise playing an increased role in our social welfare arouses strong and conflicting reactions. To a large extent, these derive from different perspectives on the preferred role of the state in providing services. For those who support social enterprise, the state forms an important and logical part of policies designed to open up, for example, health care to diverse providers.

# democratic accountability

**J**amie Oliver undeniably gained the support of millions of television viewers for his approach to the school meals problem – but how legitimate did that make him? After all, no one had elected him. This question of legitimacy is relevant to the debate on social entrepreneurship.

The government response to the social entrepreneurial approach has changed over the years. At first they thought it was a great idea, but bemoaned the lack of examples. When Community Action Network (CAN) and others started to uncover examples, and plenty of them, in estates and cities, towns and villages all over the country, government seemed pleased to see them, but remained sceptical about their overall usefulness. Now that there are many well-documented examples of their success in delivering results for the people in their areas, some described by Hazel Blears's Fabian Society pamphlet, the government focus is on their purported lack of democratic accountability.

This does not mean that the social entrepreneur should be discounted. Quite the opposite: it demonstrates an urgent need for our politicians to do the thinking required to develop a political framework that confers legitimacy on their approach. Clearly, accountable leadership needs to be encouraged in the realm of service delivery. We need to find ways of giving legitimate authority to the Jamie Olivers of this world, people with track records of delivery. We also need to consider investing in future generations of these people. They should not still be forced to face into the wind; they need to have the wind in their sails.

Several of our residents in east London, having been involved with the Centre, have themselves become actively involved in managing a housing company. They have also questioned why it is that councillors need to be on the board – seeing as some of them don't even turn up to meetings, certainly none of them have any experience running a £300 million business, and few people in the area have ever heard of or met them. Given these concerns – the lack of apparent willingness, lack of experience and lack of popularity in the area – they began to ask who these councillors actually represented; does their position necessarily confer them legitimacy? Or does real legitimacy rather lie in the hands of the people who are working on the ground, getting real and being committed? If we are to 'trust local people' we need a political framework that is robust and not naïve.

People make the assumption that simply involving more people in the decision-making process is a good thing because it is 'more democratic'. As a new life peer, I hear this argument a lot during debates about the future of the House of Lords. I have listened to all three main parties in the House of Commons arguing for a 100 per cent representative elected chamber in the Lords, believing that greater representation will be mean a more lively democracy. My point is that this has not been the case in my experience on the streets in Bromley-by-Bow – local people do not feel that they are represented. They do not feel or see the results. They do not feel empowered.

At both central and local government level, New Labour has taken steps to strengthen the power of elected leaders and enhance their ability to act decisively. There are many examples of this, but perhaps the clearest is the agenda for modernizing local government, replacing old-style council committees with a leader-and-cabinet model, in some cases with the direct election of executive mayors. In London, the successful introduction of the congestion charge needed the clear and consistent leadership of one person, the Mayor. It is hard to see how such a controversial measure would have been introduced if Ken Livingstone had been obliged to navigate through a maze of committees. Equally, the success of the London Eye, which was delivered through clear leadership from the business sector with only the lightest of touch from central and local government, offers a stark contrast with the dreadful failure of the Millennium Dome, which, though designed and constructed on time, was then ruined by the hotchpotch of exhibitions it housed, all of which were selected by committee. As the architect Richard Rogers argued at the time, the Dome was a circus in desperate need of a ringmaster.

The government's modernization of Whitehall and town hall politics is strangely at odds with the approach taken by a whole plethora of neighbourhood-based regeneration schemes, most notably the Neighbourhood Renewal Unit whose work in overseeing the government's neighbourhood renewal strategy is, as their website says, 'a continual, two-way process' between Whitehall and local government and communities (rather than being about Whitehall telling local government and communities how they should run things). At the same time as one part of government has been removing committees from town halls, another has created a massive committee infrastructure in disadvantaged neighbourhoods across the country.

I would suggest that the time has come for our politicians to put real energy into creating a political framework in which leaders like Jamie and others, who have not chosen the representative route, can be given greater legitimacy for their work. Many of them are well-respected leaders in their own communities in their own right, and have a serious track record of success. Politicians must send out absolutely clear messages that this kind of leadership must not be diluted by bureaucracy and a 'culture of committee' that imagines everyone should be consulted about everything. In return, such leaders must be expected to take personal responsibility for both their successes and their failures.

# equity

**W**e must get to grips with some of the difficulties inherent in our ideas about equity. These ideas bedevil real change in the public sector and threaten to destroy initiative and enterprise. My experience in a multicultural community in east London, where over fifty languages and dialects are spoken, suggests that admitting the world is fundamentally unfair and unequal – but full of glorious diversity – is ironically the first step to stimulating greater participation, a widening of opportunity for all and an increase in wealth creation in disadvantaged communities. Some of the mantras that underpin much traditional thinking in this area have contributed to the impoverishment of our inner cities and have undermined both community and personal responsibility. Anyone who wants to know what equality means in practice has only to look around the poor-quality housing on our estates to know just how unjust this thinking is. Here everything is fair and equal – equally mediocre. Many of the politicians who represent the residents who live in this accommodation wisely choose not to live in the midst of such conditions.

The emphasis must now be on access to opportunity, on recognizing individuals and their passions and talents and on developing these by bringing together teams of local people focused on identifiable tasks, rather than relying on representative structures. Turning passion into practice may take many forms. If an enterprise culture demands that we become more honest about the potential of the individual in their relationship to other individuals, then variety will be the spice of life.

We have found, in the East End of London, that genuine community and a sense of trust can only be created, and social capital developed, when people stop thinking in terms of the lowest common denominator. Only then do people become clear about the true nature of the world and the opportunities available to them within it. Social capital can only be created for many when we move beyond a 'theological theory' of human life and grow a strong and honest sense of belonging and community, focused around a shared practical task.

# inside the government programme

'C ommunity' has been at the heart of the New Labour project, ever since it invented itself in opposition. It sees 'community' not only as a source of social good in itself but also as a tool for regeneration and renewal in those parts of society that have been neglected for decades. Tony Blair made this the theme of his very first speech as Prime Minister, in June 1997, when he announced the possibility of a new 'alliance between the haves and the have-nots', promising that New Labour would 'find out what works... support the successes and stop the failures... back anyone – from a multinational company to a community association – if they can deliver the goods'.

His words posed a challenge by drawing attention to the work of social entrepreneurs and suggesting that power and decision-making in disadvantaged neighbourhoods might be vested in individuals or groups who 'can deliver', rather than in representative, elected committees and boards. The work of social entrepreneurs challenges the dominant notion of what constitutes democratic legitimacy. In doing so, it is honest about the failure of existing representative structures of local government to involve, or even to inter-est, the great majority of the population – in thriving as well as disadvantaged neighbourhoods. When Margaret Hodge MP publicly voiced her worry about the number of traditional white working-class voters who are turning to the BNP, rather than Westminster, for political leadership she was much criticized – but the results of the 2006 local government elections in Barking and Dagenham appeared to prove her concerns to be justified, with the BNP seizing eleven of the thirteen seats it contested. In the long term, the approach of the social entrepreneur tests the strength of New Labour's commitment to devolution. Rather than seeing devolution in terms of creating more politicians and more institutions, it involves a further redistribution of power and decision-making discretion, and a new approach to information and evaluation.

Blair's speech suggests also that resources should be directed at 'successes' and not 'failures' and so challenges traditional notions of 'equity' and 'fairness', which drive the cycles of poverty. This idea recommends that the market should be tested by taking calculated risks. It challenges existing approaches to minimizing financial risk, and questions widely accepted views of accountability. It suggests that regeneration programmes and mainstream public-sector spending programmes in disadvantaged neighbourhoods should aim to enable people living in them to create wealth for themselves and their communities rather than forever being the passive recipients of public-sector money.

The announcement in the millennium year of a Neighbourhood Renewal Fund (NRF) set the tone for the fate of Blair's initial call to arms. This fund was set up to tackle the chronic under-performance of public services in the country's most deprived neighbourhoods. NRF monies, aided and abetted by the civil service, were placed entirely in the hands of local authorities and community involvement was centred almost entirely on representation on 'Local Strategic Partnerships'. In aiming 'to help raise outcomes for those living in the most deprived neighbourhoods', government policy seemed to miss the point: it is not outcomes that need to be raised, but incomes.

About this time I was invited to a meeting at the Home Office by Lord Falconer (a close friend of Blair's and in my view a good guy). Charlie Falconer was at the time a Home Office Minister with responsibility in the area of neighbourhood renewal. In a meeting, which included the architect Lord Richard Rogers, Genie Turton, a top civil servant, and others, I argued that the time had come to take the PM's speech on the Aylesbury Estate seriously and put some real resources behind individuals and successful social entrepreneurs. Richard was very supportive and Charlie quickly agreed, saying that for too long this had been talked about and that now it was time to do it. I said at the time to Lord Falconer that my experience of government was that unless an individual was appointed to take charge of personally ensuring it actually happened, there would be little movement forward. Charlie asked me to produce a proposal, which my team and I did, enthusiastically and on deadline.

Weeks went by and nothing happened. Telephone calls were not followed through. Joe Montgomery, the head of the Neighbourhood Renewal Unit, played politics with us. And the senior civil servant who was meant to be responsible for it all could never be seen for dust. The Minister had made a serious request based on the Prime Minister's vision, yet nothing happened to see it through. There was no real personal responsibility or accountability in the system; it was as if the implied challenge to civil service structures could not be allowed to gain ground. Evasion was the name of the game – continue with business as usual. Within months Lord Falconer had been moved to another post outside the Home Office and another opportunity was lost.

This experience could be illustrated countless times over through our encounters with government in our work at the Bromley-by-Bow Centre. It actually became a source of great amusement among staff and colleagues. But it also encouraged cynicism about the New Labour project. 'Personal responsibility' and 'accountability' are words that really matter and have great meaning for social entrepreneurs; the idea that they could be applied to the New Labour government was becoming a joke. My colleagues and I now laugh about nodding dogs in car windows and the BBC series *Yes, Minister*, but in reality I watched as what little faith any of us had in the democratic process was gradually undermined. It was serious but no one seemed to care.

The Prime Minister started New Labour on the right track. His speech on the Aylesbury Estate was groundbreaking; it actually grasped the message of the social entrepreneur. But within days, as government began to focus more on management than enterprise, and more on formal representation than on direct practical involvement, whatever velocity the speech might have sparked gradually dissipated.

I was interested to read a little piece in London's *Metro* free commuter newspaper in April 2006. In the article Lord

Birt, a former Number 10 adviser, revealed how a senior civil servant toiled for six months over one page of a report on drugs. 'He justified the long delay to MPs yesterday by claiming that writing Government strategy was "hard intellectual work"'. Lord Birt was being questioned by the Commons Public Administration Committee as part of a probe into strategic thinking in government.

In the meantime, another emperor is attempting to dress in these clothes.

In the 2005 Budget, the then Chancellor of the Exchequer, Gordon Brown, announced a consultation on a Local Enterprise Growth Initiative (LEGI) to support enterprising activity and the creation of sustainable communities. Britain was told that enterprise provided local authorities with a powerful way of pursuing economic development in deprived areas. He also noted that levels of enterprise in deprived areas were significantly and persistently lower than in affluent areas. The Local Enterprise Growth Initiative would be worth £50 million in 2006–7, rising to £150 million per year by 2008–9, and would invest in and support locally developed and owned strategies that are trying out new or improved ways of stimulating economic activity, productivity and enterprise in some of the country's most deprived areas. Gordon Brown said:

> Britain is now ready for the next round of enterprise
> reforms and a step change in creating a more dynamic
> enterprise culture in our most deprived areas. We must
> ensure that there is no no-go area for enterprise in twenty-
> first century Britain. But we cannot close this gap
> overnight, nor can government do it alone. Success

depends upon innovation and creativity of both entrepreneurs and local communities themselves.

The Chancellor went on to tell us all how the LEGI would unlock the economic potential of our most deprived local areas through enterprise and investment – thereby boosting incomes and employment opportunities, building sustainable communities and helping to overcome decades of disadvantage and poor economic performance. All very wonderful stuff. How were they going to do this? Would they gather together this country's most successful business people to advise them? No. What followed was a string of command that resembled a bowl of spaghetti. The money would go from the Treasury to the Office of the Deputy Prime Minister and then on to one of the regional government offices. They, in turn, would give money to local authorities, at which point,

> There will be agreements struck between Government, the
> local authority and its major delivery partners in an area…
> Local Area Agreements will be driven by the local authority
> with Local Strategic Partnerships (to ensure engagement of
> local partners). Negotiations will be overseen by the
> respective Government Office and signed off by Ministers.

So, eventually, the money goes to Local Strategic Partnerships. But who are these eminent bodies? And what do they do? For a start, they are not local. They are borough wide. Because they are borough wide, they are not 'strategic' and certainly not 'partnerships' in any business sense of that word. They are not run well; they are heavily dominated by statutory bodies and they have particular problems in engaging with the business community. I for one do not see them creating a more dynamic enterprise culture in our most deprived areas. The proposal continued, stirring the spaghetti once more:

Local authorities will develop local proposals for enterprise. These proposals should then form part of the wider Community Strategy. They would work closely with local partners and the Regional Development Agencies (RDAs). They would develop a local evidence base to inform decision-making. They will determine both the appropriate local indicators to pursue and the actions (or policies) required to meet them. They will integrate the wider efforts including neighbourhood renewal; and set challenging outcome-focused targets to incentives delivery and secure value for money. These factors will then be considered by Government Offices when assessing individual applications for LEGI support. Any local proposals in the field of economic development will need to fit with the broader Regional Economic Strategy (RES) developed by the RDA. Local authorities should therefore work in partnership with RDAs not only to ensure there is congruence with the RES, but that complementarities and synergies are taken advantage of, combining resources where possible and appropriate.

This is 100 per cent process. Five hundred million pounds of public money wasted, most of it going on the salaries of civil servants, university academics and government bureaucracy. This is another proverbial turkey twizzler served up yet again in Britain's poorest communities. I suspect the people I have been concerned about in this book will actually see little of this resource and Margaret Hodge will continue to worry about why white working-class voters are becoming disillusioned with New Labour. As I observe the government processes that are meant to deliver an Olympic legacy on our doorstep in the Lower Lea Valley, a very similar tale appears about to be repeated in the countless strategies and plans that are appearing on my desk. But more of that later.

In 2002 I was invited to become an associate member of the Prime Minister's Delivery Unit (PMDU), charged with improving the delivery of public services. At the first meeting it became clear that it was a classic academic arrangement. We were told about eighty categories of targets which would in turn check that delivery targets in all the main government programmes were being met in every hospital and school and organ of public service across the land. When I asked at one of the early meetings how we could be confident about the figures collected, and how we could be sure that they were accurately measuring what was really going on at the school in Darnell in Sheffield, there was a great shuffling of chairs at the front and a veritable rash of uncomfortable glances exchanged. Another associate said that she had just read their report on the accident and emergency unit in Barnsley – which seemed on the surface to be an excellent report, detailing a real improvement in service. However, when she actually visited the hospital she discovered a rundown environment, in which corridors were being counted as wards and trolleys were being counted as beds.

A great deal can happen in the sixty thousand feet that separate the NHS office in Whitehall from that hospital in Barnsley. The people in the middle of the supply chain are experts in running the systems and processes that provide both civil servants and politicians with exactly the data and information they require to help them sleep soundly in their beds at night. But do these figures bear any relationship to reality? Is this why at the 2006 Royal College of Nurses conference, Health Secretary Patricia Hewitt was jeered and slow-handclapped by the delegates? What Patricia sees on the papers in front of her and what the nurses are actually facing on the wards are two different worlds, yet politicians look mystified at all the fuss. After all, they have read the numbers, they know the 'facts'. Would an entrepreneur even want to join this merry-go-round? I think not. Gordon Brown's eighty-two-page document on enterprise seemed woefully short of the merest practical clue about how to deliver results!

So enough moaning. What would I suggest? Lord Peyton would often tell me that if you couldn't put it on a side of A4, then it wasn't up to much. He reminded me that if Winston Churchill, who he had known, could plot out the Second World War on the back of an envelope, then setting out an enterprise initiative for poor communities would be a doddle. Now Gordon Brown is Prime Minister, my advice to him is this: forget the Rowntree reports into the results of your own policies. Follow the detail from top to bottom.

# words of caution

I want to encourage people to dump much of the more ideological thinking that they have picked up over the years
and to embrace instead more practical responses to
some of the UK's most challenging social questions. I argue
for a practical approach based around 'learning by doing'
and encouraging people to 'get their hands dirty', and
remain sceptical about a culture that makes few demands
on the individual and is dominated by policy papers and
academic theory – precisely the world that underpins much
of the current way of 'doing government', and a methodology which has been found to be far from effective the world
over. This is where the answer to the democratic deficit is
likely to be found, not in playing around with a British constitution, and worrying about the future of the House of
Lords. Such activity will simply distract us all from the heart
of the problem. It will prevent us once again from finding
solutions that encourage greater local participation in our
society.

Lord Peyton, a wise old bird, an experienced politician
and former government minister, told me once that 'government often knows the shape of the forest but it has no idea
what is actually going on under the trees'. I want to show

that what is going on 'under the trees' can no longer be dismissed or ignored by any government: this very detail is the seed-bed of change. I challenge much of the traditional thinking about a political culture that believes that it both sees and understands the world by sitting in front of a computer screen. History suggests that bringing about real, sustainable change involves practical experience, human hardship and personal sacrifice.

I have gleaned enormous personal satisfaction from being committed to London's East End over many years, by rolling up my sleeves and getting stuck into all the messy detail over a long period of time. My family has benefited from this long-term relationship as well. It has certainly been difficult but, over time, it is hugely rewarding. This kind of long-term commitment to an area can create a strong community within which we can support each other, and within which we can all thrive.

I seek not only to influence government thinking on the debate about social enterprise that is currently raging across all three major political parties in Britain today but also to warn all our political leaders of the dangers of trying to grab at every new idea in town. I want to discourage too much political interference, encourage politicians to slow down – their role should be in creating a rich environment and level playing field on which social enterprise can flourish; and then to back off.

I am reminded of the housing association movement that started to blossom in the sixties. This movement began in an entrepreneurial way and produced many excellent practical examples of innovation in social housing. These small and very special housing associations, one of which I was

Secretary of for a time, produced some quality buildings and paid the necessary attention to detail which real innovation demands. But when government got involved and created the Housing Corporation, bringing in a civil-service culture to adjudicate on matters, these smaller shoots were suffocated with bureaucracy, audit trails and government structures. Now the situation truly was all equal: equally mediocre.

If you visit some of the flats that are currently being built by housing associations in some of our poorest neighbourhoods, you can see the next phase of poverty housing being built, at great public expense, right before your eyes – housing which looks very much like the kinds of housing their forerunners, the local authority housing departments, had produced many years earlier. Think Dagenham. This is happening despite all the government rhetoric about quality design and the establishment of the Commission for Architecture and the Built Environment (CABE) to monitor the quality of the built environment in this country. Of course, there are notable exceptions, like Coin Street on the South Bank of the Thames (built by the social entrepreneur Ian Tuckett), but I would be willing to bet that where they are to be found, they are headed up by an individual who, like Ian, has stayed the course over many years (over twenty years in Ian's case, running Coin Street Community Builders).

I believe that the government should put less blind faith in system and process, but offer us more opportunities to take more personal responsibility for social issues. I would like to see a serious overhaul of the civil service and its prevailing culture, which infects every bit of the public sector and so often undermines real change. I believe that it is individuals who change the world (some of whom are in the civil service – I have met them) and that the key lies in identifying these change-makers and supporting them wholeheartedly. It is *people* who make all the difference and I worry that so many policy papers fail to even mention them.

The social enterprise movement today faces the same dangers as those faced in the middle of the last century by the housing association movement. I fear that if we are not careful, those who too eagerly embrace the government mindset will find themselves signing the death warrant of a new movement.

Despite the rhetoric, very little actually changed during the Blair years. The Bromley-by-Bow Centre sits at the heart of a group of rundown estates in the East End of London. Despite all the government rhetoric about 'joined-up' think-ing and 'joined-up' action, the Centre still faces the gruelling task of having to administer seventy-seven different funding sources, emanating from a range of different government departments, all demanding their outputs, evaluation pro-cedures and audit trails. When I mentioned this fact recently to the cabinet minister Hilary Armstrong MP, when she visited the Centre with four other government ministers to launch the government's Social Exclusion Action Plan, she was shocked – but she did not do anything about it. Ultimately, she took no personal responsibility for an uncomfortable fact, despite telling us in her speech that she wanted to see 'more Bromley-by-Bows around the country'.

Social entrepreneurs everywhere are finding that deliver-ing results in practice has become harder, not easier. I want to talk about the realities that we face on the ground, and try to unravel and begin to understand them from the inside. To do this, it is necessary to ask some difficult questions about why the New Labour government – which came to power with such a democratic mandate – has not been able to deliver enough real change; why social entrepreneurs remain so unconvinced by their actions; and how far the 'macro' policy emanating from the hothouse of Downing Street is disconnected from the 'micro' realities three miles up the road in the heart of some of the United Kingdom's most difficult housing estates.

Government should not be grabbing at every new idea or attempting to fix every social problem – evidence suggests they often make things worse by doing this. Their role is to create the conditions for change – to create a marketplace for social and business entrepreneurs that encourages them to work together and interact. In order to achieve this, they must open up the public sector in far more radical ways than they have as yet attempted. They must remove the public sector from its privileged position, get rid of the merry-go-round of local authority officers shifting from job to job within the authority, and bring in new blood, people who have cut their teeth on entrepreneurial environments. Change is all about having the right people in the right places – forget about endless restructuring and new processes. The NHS has been through over twenty restructures during the years I have been working with it. This can't be a healthy way to proceed, not for the people involved or the individuals who rely on its services.

The question of whether it is the role of the state to deliver change on the ground or to provide the resources for others to do so promises to be an area of fierce debate during the next general election in this country. When things are working well it is fine for business and social enterprise to deliver public services, but should the state intervene when things are going wrong? Delivering genuine transformation is a risky business and all governments struggle with it. However, unless governments take the long view, and withdraw and provide genuine space for social entrepreneurs to operate – and, yes, at times fail – real change will never happen.

# TWELVE STEPS TOWARDS AN ENTREPRENEURIAL FUTURE

## One

The Bromley-by-Bow Centre works because we have put a lot of effort into understanding an area and the people who live there over many years. It is important to understand that in the early days social innovation demanded that we learn to 'play' with ideas and to experiment with new ways of working without fully understanding where they would lead or what structure and form they would eventually take. Only as we gained practical experience and matured as an organization did we begin to develop structural forms, much of them drawn from business, which enabled us to grow the organization. Rob Trimble, our CEO today, is from a business background and has taken this early work and developed it even further, being in the process of growing one of the most dynamic social businesses in the UK. The work that Rob is leading in Bromley-by-Bow is about combining a sure-footed and clear-headed business approach with our constant belief in local people and their ability to transform their lives, their families and their community.

Over the years we have tried very hard to be honest and trusting with each other, as one human being to another. Our concern to create a community based on these principles has paid off and we, in turn, are generally trusted by the local community – not least because we are a visible part of it.

It is telling that, almost without exception, whenever we have applied for funding from statutory agencies, we have felt there to be no interest or desire to get really involved and connected; no thought of getting properly engaged and forging a relationship with us and our community. It has all been about the written word.

If you want to engage with communities, you need to build long-term relationships and gain the trust of the people, and the best way to achieve this is to get on with practical project work based on the realities of people's daily lives, which you commit to seeing through to the end. Simply establishing representative structures, which politicize communities, is not helpful.

## Two

There is a whole swathe of reports trying to define what a social enterprise is, how many there are, or whether you can allow them market capital. Millions of pounds of public money are being spent on churning out these reports. But, for me, they entirely miss the point. Social entrepreneurs are to be found in *all* sectors of our society – in business, in the voluntary sector, in the public sector; on the high street and in the boardroom and in ordinary living rooms up and down the country. They are difficult to define precisely *because* they are being entrepreneurial – and the moment you define and categorize entrepreneurship, it will shift shape and render your definition obsolete. If it works, it works, no matter how you're defining it.

## Three

Like talks to like – bureaucrats talk to bureaucracies. By contracting out many public services, New Labour – quite rightly, in my opinion – attempted to bring new energy into the provision of public-sector services. However, the reality saw the migration of civil servants across into the business sector: they effectively ended up running the same services they had previously, but wearing a private-sector hat. What was private sector in name, therefore, simply became public sector one step removed. Previously dynamic organizations were taken over by the logic of the state. This will not encourage change – quite the opposite. Politicians need to ensure real innovation takes place.

We must also be suspicious of large consultancies with well-known brands who earn millions of pounds from government by telling them often what they think they want to hear. I've often seen these firms produce long and very expensive reports that the famous fictional East Ender Alf Garnett (from *'Til Death Do Us Part*) would have dubbed as 'statements of the bleedin' obvious'. Such bodies would be well advised to work closely with social entrepreneurs to discover genuine new approaches to social problems and not simply regurgitate old solutions that civil servants can feel comfortable with. One business colleague described this approach as 'blotting paper down the trousers'! There is considerable room for innovation here if government gives the right signals and encourages innovative partnerships between business and social entrepreneurs.

## Four

Support the Social Venture Capital movement. One of the

most significant changes of the last twenty years in Britain has been the massive increase in the number of seriously wealthy individuals. Many of them, along with their associated companies and corporations, want to move beyond traditional philanthropy by investing their time in, and applying their business skills to, tackling social problems. The Impetus Trust is one example; Community Action Network's partnership with Primera and Sony is another. Interestingly, however, it is far harder to find evidence of smaller-scale private entrepreneurs engaging with social enterprise. This is a real gap, which should be plugged.

## Five

Government has a tendency to behave as if the way to understand a local community is by representative committee, established to discuss with 'the people' what should happen in their area. It sounds good, but there is another more effective way to engage with a local population. In Bromley-by-Bow, rather than invite people to discuss what should happen in, for example, the park, we invited people along and literally gave them the tools to rebuild it.

We had a rule in the early days: if someone came forward with an idea we would not, if at all possible, say 'write a proposal for the management committee'. Instead, we'd tell them to get on with it. As you've seen, this is how so many of our most successful initiatives began. A whole bunch of artist entrepreneurs started this way, as did the two disability organizations, as did Green Dreams, the gardening business. Just get stuck in and give it a go, was our feeling. Of course, hundreds of ideas went nowhere – but they *did* lead to new relationships and the burgeoning of a positive 'learning by doing' culture.

If you are from a secure family and a well-educated background, with a bit of money, a bit of self-esteem and some contacts, you are lucky. In an area like Bromley-by-Bow, nearly everything is run by the state – housing, health, the money in your pocket, whether your children live with you or not. Nearly everything requires a form from somewhere or other to be filled in, signed, stamped, considered, responded to... The contrast between that kind of an experience of life – which, believe me, can feel frustrating and actively discouraging – and someone simply saying, 'Sure, go ahead, when can you start and how can we help?', without forms or systems or anything else, just a person talking face to face with another person, is not to be underestimated.

## Six
Allow leaders to be leaders. There is a natural geography of power. This kind of authority isn't taken, it is given and it is earned. The true social entrepreneur is given power by others. Think Jamie Oliver. Or Bob Geldof.

## Seven
Government needs to be clear and definitive on what it will *not* fund. Only then will everyone feel more confident about what funds *will* actually be spent on.

## Eight
Government needs to focus on getting the detail of effective delivery of social and public services right, rather than

simply focusing on an overall 'goal' or 'objective'. It needs to ask itself: who in the world is the best person, with practical experience, to make this venture work? Is he or she working in a key position on government reform? If not, why not?

## Nine

Develop smarter ways of engaging with the private and social sector together. There are some good examples. At Stanton Guildhouse we have a partnership with Rural Retreats, a national business which provides holiday lets in beautiful houses to families and couples. We formed a business relationship with them and they offer Stanton Guildhouse through their marketing brochure to over 250,000 people across the UK and beyond for the holiday weeks and weekends when we are not using the house. The social enterprise earns a realistic fee for this service which supports our other work with more vulnerable communities. There is still a divide between bidding rounds for the social sector and tendering for the private sector when the most effective solution could well require that the two sectors work together.

## Ten

Don't buy process: buy results. New technology means that it is increasingly possible to more or less measure the outcomes of particular projects – on people's health, educational achievement, levels of participation... So why not use it?

## Eleven

Build on the people and the approaches that work. For all its flaws, the National Institute for Clinical Excellence (NICE) at least attempts to produce evidence of what is effective and what is not and to make clinical health policy recommendations based on this evidence. However, there is little to show that this approach is being taken elsewhere in government, which is a shame. There is very little hard evidence of the effectiveness of this kind of approach, but I would be willing to bet that if there were, it would be encouraging.

## Twelve

Be clear about accountability. The belief that a committee is more accountable than an individual should be seriously challenged. When an individual takes a decision, be it a head teacher, a minister, or a clergyman in a rundown East End estate, they are visible. Give more personal responsibility and hold individuals to account for what they do. This is difficult in a culture that has chosen to go down the legislative route of human rights. The litigiousness which results from it breaks down relationships and severs the bonds of trust that make any community possible. It will, I believe, bring with it a terrible price and fracture some of Britain's poorest communities.

Being clearer about what government is doing, what it is not doing, and having individuals visibly responsible for more clearly defined tasks – as well as efficient, effective measurement of outcomes – will mean less paperwork, less confusion and more accountability.

# WHAT NEXT FOR EAST LONDON?

# water city

n 1999, as the Centre was beginning to grow, I became aware that there was some talk of the possibility of the Olympics coming to London in 2012. I was equally aware that probably the only place they could take place was the Lower Lea Valley, at the heart of which was Bromley-by-Bow. This was the only area in the capital where there was still enough land. I met with Paul Brickell and Richard Sumray, the indefatigable champion of a London Olympic bid who was at the time with London Sport International, to discuss what seemed to us to be a momentous opportunity. If the Olympics ever did come our way, they could act as a powerful catalyst for east London. A big occasion required a big idea.

Fly into London City Airport and look down. All you can see is water – the river Thames, river Lea, the many interconnecting canals and the huge expanse of water of the Royal Docks. They hold amazing potential to lift the quality of life of this woefully rundown part of the city that my colleagues and I have invested ourselves in over so many years, but this potential has never been fully grasped. Until now. Our idea was to rediscover these rivers, canals and docks – from Canary Wharf to the Royal Docks and from

Greenwich to Hackney Marshes – and create a fantastic place to live and work; a Water City. And the Olympics would be the catalyst.

Following our conversations, Paul and I joined Richard in floating the idea of the Olympics and east London with colleagues. I am sure many of them thought we were mad and some in the public sector were very clear that this was not for them. I decided to go and see the architect Richard Rogers, who I knew, and test the water with a serious player. Paul, Richard and I met at the House of Lords some weeks later and, to my surprise, Richard had not the slightest hesitation in agreeing that what we were suggesting, a 'Water City', was a great idea and timely. I knew we were on to something. Richard agreed to gather together a team to help us work on the project, and we were off. Our small team of enthusiasts wrote what was to become the first booklet on the London Olympics. In it, we positioned the idea of a Water City at the core of the Olympic project.

Over four hundred years ago a Dutch engineer dreamed of building a network of canals across the desolate marshlands of the Lower Lea Valley in order to bring prosperity to the scattered hamlets of east London. Two hundred years passed before these dreams became a reality and the docks and waterways of the river Thames and river Lea began to power the economy of east London – literally, in the case of the eighteenth-century House Mill, which still stands in Bromley-by-Bow. It harnessed the energy of the tides to grind grain which had been carried down the river in barges from the countryside to provide the raw material for the production of alcohol, which was used both for industrial and recreational consumption.

When the docks, mills, distilleries and factories began to close thirty years ago, the waterways became derelict and forgotten and merely added to the fragmentation and disconnection of the neighbourhoods along their banks.

Our vision is to rediscover the rivers, canals and docks of east London, and create a Water City for the twenty-first century which will be a fantastic place in which to live and to work. Our aim is to capture the entrepreneurial energy of east London's remarkable communities and to enable them to co-create the Water City with the world's finest architects, designers and economists, and in the process transform the economic opportunities and life chances of east Londoners for ever.

Creating the Water City is a forty-year task at least. It requires vision, belief, hard work and a lot of investment. East London has come a long way over the past twenty years, but it still has a long way still to go. Major new developments are getting under way at Stratford City around the new international station, at Silvertown Quays and at Canning Town, which will include Biota!, a stunning new aquatic life centre. A new network of bridges can also begin connecting disconnected pieces of the city, crossing the roads, railways and waterways that carve their way through our neighbourhoods.

And in the middle of all of this redevelopment come the 2012 Olympic and Paralympic Games – a global extravaganza in our back yard. We all hope that 2012 will bring a haul of medals and prizes for our athletes. This will be one important measure of whether the 2012 Olympiad turns out, in Lord Coe's words, to be 'the best Games ever'. However, for us who live and work in east London, the

Games are an important opportunity to both hasten and enhance the physical transformation of east London, as well as to showcase the extraordinary richness of its cultures and the energy and creativity of its people. In this lies the chance to realise the bid's promised legacy for the arts, health, education, skills, jobs and business development.

We could produce one of the first Olympic Games in history that actually delivers on its promised legacy of sustainable physical, social and economic regeneration, and we could use the preparation for the Games to explore how to marry central policy and local delivery effectively. 'Stage the Olympic Games' is a heavy-duty central policy directive, but there can be no legacy unless this is integrated closely with local planning and sustained, effective local delivery. How to integrate the central and the local – Whitehall and neighbourhoods - is one of the main unsolved policy conundrums of New Labour, affecting all areas of public service. Let the Olympics give us the courage and imagination to address it.

The Olympic Games will bring to east London about £9 billion of investment. This is indeed a great deal of money. But put together all the planned developments on the Greenwich Peninsula, at Silvertown Quays, the Royal Docks, Canning Town, Stratford City and elsewhere, and you get a figure of over £20 billion of investment coming into the area over the next twenty years. This is the *real* legacy: and the Olympic and Paralympic Games in 2012 are a tremendous catalyst that can kick it into action. This is a unique opportunity for east Londoners to reconnect with their past and to use this historic asset of the water once again to drive the economic regeneration of the area, creating an 'Amsterdam in London' and transforming the area for generations to come.

The question is: will the Mayor of London, the London Development Agency and London Thames Gateway Development Corporation; the Olympics Delivery Authority and the London Organising Committee for the Olympic Games, and the politicians who oversee various public-sector bodies, be able to build on the knowledge and many years of experience that already exists at the heart of the Lower Lea Valley? Or will they go it alone? Will they believe that they are the 'only show in town', until the next government restructuring comes along, or will they join forces with the long-term players and local communities in which they work, building on the hard-won experience of social entrepreneurs who have worked in the valley for many years?

Major businesses and London's global academic institutions are coming to understand the potential of this opportunity, and are working with social entrepreneurs and with civic entrepreneurs in the London Borough of Newham to find ways of realizing it. Will government and public-sector bodies come to see that their methods of working alone will not unlock the potential? Before it is too late, will they realize that it is a business-led approach that will achieve the transformation to the 'Amsterdam of London'? Time and history will tell.

As I hope this book has shown, organic growth that puts people at its heart has a way of mushrooming. It is an idea central to Water City. Our experience has demonstrated a unique, socially entrepreneurial approach to regeneration which brings together experienced practitioners from both the business community and the social sector, and which has the potential to create a real long-term legacy. It is an idea that has global implications.

Social entrepreneurs are posing a direct and exciting challenge to the way our country is run and our cities are built. As government spends millions of pounds worrying about an Olympic legacy and how to create one, my team and I have done just that – created a positive legacy for a previously neglected community – just two hundred yards down the road. Social entrepreneurs up and down this land have been learning how to do this for many years. Will government engage with this hard-won experience? Watch this space.

# further reading and resources

## Andrew Mawson Partnerships

Today, I concentrate on a number of major projects as leader, motivator and adviser. I recently founded Andrew Mawson Partnerships, an informal network of highly experienced social entrepreneurs, as a vehicle for this work.

**www.amawsonpartnerships.com**

## Bromley-by-Bow Centre

The Bromley-by-Bow Centre sits two hundred yards away from the Olympic site. When I arrived there I was greeted by a derelict church, twelve elderly church members and a bank account with £400 in it. Today the three-acre site houses the first integrated health complex of its kind in the country, a new landscaped park, a 'communiversity', with a student body of over seven hundred, and a business centre working with over twenty-two social enterprises across Tower Hamlets. We employ over a hundred and forty staff on our site and have gained an international reputation for excellence in community regeneration. Through its influence, many in the local population move on from unemployment and apathy to embrace a rich new future for them and their families.

**www.bbbc.org.uk**

## Community Action Network

Founded in 1998, Community Action Network (CAN) was the vision of three innovators of social change. The founding partners were myself, Adele Blakebrough, who pioneered the Kaleidoscope project – a unique community response to drug treatment – and Helen Taylor Thompson, who founded the Mildmay Mission Hospital.

CAN helps social entrepreneurs to scale up their businesses and maximize their social impact in two ways. Firstly, CAN is an award-winning, sustainable social enterprise providing high-quality shared office accommodation for the third sector – space is sold on a per desk basis for as little as three months at a time. We offer 414 desk spaces over three floors at the Mezzanine London Bridge, and 281 desks at a second location in Southwark. Between them, these offices house some of the world's leading organizations in social change.

Secondly, we offer a range of funding options and business support for social enterprises. We run a pioneering social investment programme specifically designed to tackle the financial and management challenges that many social enterprises find standing in their way.

**www.can-online.org.uk**

## Poplar HARCA

Surrounding the Bromley-by-Bow Centre, the social housing company Poplar HARCA has assumed control of over six thousand properties from the Tower Hamlets Housing Department, and is about to take control of a further two and a half thousand properties. Thousands of local residents have chosen to opt out of council control

and join the company. Seventy-eight per cent of them chose this path in a stock transfer ballot with a 63 per cent turnout – an endorsement any politician would die for. There is an opportunity here not only to transform the area but also to connect community development to housing development. For residents, regeneration will be very real.
**www.poplarharca.co.uk**

## Leaside Regeneration Ltd
Leaside Regeneration was founded nine years ago on the initiative of Tower Hamlets Council and brought together a network of partners from the business, public and social enterprise sectors. They came together and created a company that spanned the Lower Lea Valley and, for the first time, brought together politicians across what was a historical dividing line between Newham and Tower Hamlets. Together they developed a £100 million regeneration programme stretching down the valley. One example of their success has been the completion of a new DLR station at Langdon Park, connecting a forgotten group of housing estates to the outside world.
**www.leasideregeneration.com**

## Stanton Guildhouse
Stanton Guildhouse is a beautiful stone manor house set in the Cotswolds overlooking the Vale of Evesham. It was hand-built in the sixties, in the Arts and Crafts tradition, using reclaimed Cotswold stone, former flagstones from the streets of London and beams crafted from oaks on the Blenheim Palace Estate. The interior of the house features many examples of fine craftsmanship.

It was created by Mary Osborn, a pioneer 'social entrepreneur' who came to Stanton from the East End of London and who dedicated her life to the promotion of learning, creativity and personal development. The house is associated with many of Mary Osborn's supporters, including Mahatma Gandhi, John Betjeman, Flora Robson, J. B. Priestley and Enid Blyton.

I took over responsibility for its future development in 1996, and Stanton Guildhouse is now a fully-fledged social enterprise, run on business principles with a clear social purpose. It is a charitable trust which reinvests any profit into community support and social entrepreneurial activity to improve the quality of life for those in the inner city and the countryside.

Stanton Guildhouse provides access to the peace, tranquillity and creative energy of the house and rural surroundings for local people, for inner city projects and for major businesses.

**www.stantonguildhouse.org.uk**

## Water City

East London – from Hackney Marshes and the Olympic Park in the north, down the Lower Lea Valley through Bow and Poplar to Canning Town, the Royal Docks and the Greenwich Peninsula in the south – is leaving its troubled past behind. The area now offers a tremendous development opportunity which takes advantage of the East End's greatest natural resource: its plentiful supply of water.

The Water City Group (comprising social entrepreneurs and community businesses operating in the Lower Lea Valley) and Arup, the engineering, design and management consultancy, have developed a proposal for Water City as London's Olympic legacy for the whole of the Lower Lea Valley.

This proposal reflects the fact that the time is right for developing an integrated strategy for the regeneration of the Water City area which builds on the London 2012 Olympic and Paralympic Games. This strategy identifies and addresses the social, economic and environmental objectives for the region – and how they should be delivered.
**www.watercity.org.uk**

## St Paul's Way

St Paul's Way runs through the heart of Poplar in the East End and lies in the midst of Europe's largest regeneration area. Within a few hundred yards of each other along St Paul's Way are two housing estates, a secondary school, two primary schools, a GP surgery, a retail parade and several community facilities. Yet far from bringing communities together, St Paul's Way acts as a traffic-congested boundary between the residential communities on either side.

The St Paul's Way Transformational Project was conceived in early 2006 with the aim of bringing a coordinated neighbourhood approach to the regeneration of the area. Shortly afterwards the St Paul's Way Partnership was created, bringing together the London Borough of Tower Hamlets, Tower Hamlets PCT and Poplar HARCA. I am the project's director.

Our aim is to transform not only the physical environment along St Paul's Way, but also the relationships between the various service providers along the street, and between fragmented local communities.
**www.stpaulsway.org.uk**

## Silvertown Quays

Silvertown Quays is a major £1.5 billion development that is beginning to take shape alongside the impressive waterfront of the Royal Docks on the river Thames in east London.

This waterside regeneration development will include five thousand new homes (including over 1,300 affordable units), 7,800 square metres of office space and 7,600 square metres of flexible workspace, together with community facilities, restaurants, bars and leisure facilities. At its heart will be Biota!, the world's first aquatic visitor attraction to be based entirely on the principles of conservation. Expected to attract over one million visitors a year, Biota! will be operated by the Zoological Society of London and will include scientific research, education and breeding projects, with a direct link to field conservation programmes.

**www.silvertownquays-london.com**

## The NHS LIFT programme

The aim of the NHS Local Improvement Finance Trust (LIFT) programme is to construct new facilities for the provision of new forms of primary health and social care services, particularly in parts of the country where the health of the population is relatively poor. The programme was launched in 2001 and now operates in forty-two areas across the UK. The programme is delivered through local LIFT companies. These are public-private sector partnership companies whose shareholders include Primary Care Trusts, UK government (via Partnerships for Health), private sector partners identified through competitive procurement and, in some cases, local authorities. The UK's first NHS LIFT

company was East London LIFTCo and the first new facility was opened in East Ham in Newham in 2004.
**www.partnershipsforhealth.co.uk**

## One Church 100 Uses

There are an increasing number of churches with small congregations which are no longer, or will shortly cease to be, viable. This is the experience of all the Christian denominations in the UK.

The United Reformed Church has recently created One Church 100 Uses, a Community Interest Company designed to tackle this issue head on by providing specialist property and regeneration expertise to local churches.

As a regeneration agency within the United Reformed Church, One Church 100 Uses will put in place a plan which will redevelop church premises and then hand them over to a local church or agency, whilst allowing the United Reformed Church to retain ownership of the property. This approach is ecumenical, rooted in its local context and sustainable. For each situation there will be a solution which is financially, socially and spiritually beneficial.
**www.onechurch100uses.co.uk**

## Publications

*There's No Business Like Social Business: How to be Socially Enterprising* by Liam Black and Jeremy Nicholls (The Cats Pyjama's, 2004)

*The Rise of the Social Entrepreneur* by Charles Leadbeater (Demos, 1997)

*People Before Structures* by Paul Brickell (Demos, 2000)

# acknowledgements

I would like to thank all those colleagues who have helped me with this book and who supported me through this challenging process. I would particularly like to thank Paul Brickell, Donald Findley, Rob Trimble and Colin Bayley for helping me with the text, Toby Mundy, Sarah Castleton and the team at Atlantic Books for being so patient and all the staff, friends and users of the Bromley-by-Bow Centre who have provided me with so much of the material.